The On-line

Business

Survival Guide

Featuring

The Wall Street Journal Interactive Edition.

John Wiley & Sons, Inc.
New York • Chichester • Weinheim • Brisbane • Singapore • Toronto

ISBN 0-471-32738-7

Printed in the United States of America

10 9 8 7 6 5 4

Printed and bound by Hamilton Printing Company

Table of Contents

Chapter 1
What You Need to Start

Topics

- Introduction
- Basic Computer Configuration
- Modem
- Internet Software
- Internet Service Provider

Introduction

This book provides students with a basic introduction to doing business research on the Internet with particular emphasis on *The Wall Street Journal Interactive Edition*®. Though it is by no means the only site available for students to do this kind of research, the *Interactive Journal* receives special attention here because it is one of the better locations for conducting business research and because many students will have access to the site at some point during their education.

Students who have previous experience "surfing the net" may not need to read all of the chapters here. For example, Chapter 1 describes the basic computer configuration that you need to successfully navigate on the Internet, as well as some of the different types of Internet service providers available in today's marketplace. Chapter 2 describes the structure of the Internet and illustrates how to use Netscape, perhaps the most widely used Web browser. If your school provides the hardware you need, and you have used Netscape or any other browser in the past, you can skip right to Chapter 3. There you will learn about search engines, perhaps the most fundamental tool you need to do research on the Internet. The chapter describes several different types of search engines and illustrates briefly how to use a few of them.

Chapter 4 provides in depth coverage of the resources available from the *Interactive Journal*. If you have access to this site and plan to use it to prepare reports for class or to do research on your own, you'll want to invest some time reading through this chapter. It's best to do so while you're on the Web, so you can see for yourself how the site works. Chapter 4 offers several examples of the kinds of questions that the *Interactive Journal* can help you answer, but the site has so much to offer that this book really just gives you an introduction.

Having done some research on the Web, you might want to publish it by creating your own Web page. Chapter 5 provides a brief introduction to Hypertext Markup Language (HTML), the language of the Web. You can create your own page from scratch by learning HTML, or you may opt to purchase a Web publishing software package that will handle the technical side of this process for you. The best and the worst thing about the Internet is the vast amount of information available to anyone with a computer and browser. You can find just about anything, but there is so much available that finding just what you need can sometimes be a challenge. In the final chapter, we offer a list of web sites that we believe are among the best for retrieving business information.

Basic Computer Configuration

Computer Speed. A computer with a speed of Pentium 90 MHz or higher is required because many sites contain a considerable amount of graphics that must be downloaded into your computer. With a computer speed of at least Pentium 90 MHz, you will not be penalized in terms of time by the large amount of graphics.

Operating System. A Windows 3.1 operating system is sufficient. However, if you plan to get a new computer, I highly suggest Windows 95, as many new software programs are designed to run on the Windows 95 platform.

RAM. Random access memory minimum should be 16 Mb. The larger the RAM, the faster and easier it is to download graphics without freezing your computer. Having less than 16 Mb can significantly impede your surfing ability.

Monitor. A high-quality computer monitor (SVGA) is recommended for viewing high quality graphics and color on the Web. Some sites are so colorful and graphics-oriented that if you use a lower quality monitor (VGA), the content might be undecipherable.

Hard Disk Space. 8 Megabytes (MB) or 8 times 1024 bytes of hard disk space is the minimum, but your computer needs at least 10 to 15 MB of free hard disk space to run the Windows operating system properly. Therefore, do not fill up your drive to the limit. Doing so will drastically slow down your computer.

Modem. The modem is a piece of hardware that allows your computer to dial and connect with a network provider (we will discuss this in the next section). Most new computers sold today have built-in modems with speed of 14,400 Kbps (kilobits per second) or faster. I advise that you utilize a faster 28,800 Kbps modem. However, there is no need to buy a modem that is even faster than 28,800 Kbps, as local telephone lines cannot carry greater speeds than that. An exception is the new 56,000 Kbps modem which uses software technology to increase the speed of data download. The downside of this modem is that the network provider must also have the software installed in its servers. So before shelling out $200, check with your Internet service provider (ISP).

Internet Software. Of the handful of Internet software programs available in the market today, Netscape Navigator and Microsoft Internet Explorer are the most common. Windows 3.1 phone dialer software uses your modem and phone line to dial the Internet special system software (called TCPIP) which, in turn, lets your computer talk to other computers over the Internet. All of this software and installation should be provided by your ISP (see below).

Summary

Computer Type	PC-Compatible
Computer Speed	Pentium 90 MHz or better
Operating System	Windows 3.1 / Windows 95
RAM Size	16 MB
Monitor	SVGA
Hardisk Space	8 MB +
Modem	28.8 Kbps
Software	Netscape Navigator & TCPIP

Internet Service Providers

Network providers or Internet service providers (ISPs) are companies that complete the dial-up connection between your computer's modem and the Internet so that you can surf the Web, read newsgroups, and send and receive e-mail. These companies provide services that range from free software to free magazine subscriptions such as *Business Week Online* (through American Online). Before you sign up with an ISP, you should ask the following:

✓ **Should I opt for payment by the hour or for unlimited service?**

> For those of us who anticipate surfing the Web for a couple of hours a day, we recommend getting an unlimited service account. Services that charge you for the amount of time you remain on-line can become very expensive.

✓ **How many hours of free testing time can I get?**

Most ISPs give you free trial service of at least a few hours. I suggest taking advantage of this free trial to help you select your ISP. You can make your decision by doing the following test:

- Try to connect three times in a row within an hour. Make sure that you do not get more than one busy signal. If you do, get another ISP.

- Try connecting at 7:00 p.m. (Internet rush hour) to determine how many times you need to call to get a connection. If it takes more than three calls, find another ISP.

- What kind of Internet software do they use? If it is not Netscape or Microsoft Internet Explorer, find another ISP.

- Do you like their e-mail software? Test it by sending a message to yourself.

- Test the speed of graphic dowloading by checking out the sites in Chapter 6.

- Call the technical number to find out if you are able to speak with a human on the other end of the line. You will be surprised to find that often you are not.

✓ **Do they charge a setup fee?**

Some ISPs offer very low monthly fees, but kill you with the setup charge. Some charge as high as $80, so make sure you ask.

✓ **Do they have a local number in your area?**

Some nationwide Internet providers serve only large metropolises such as Los Angeles and New York. If you would have to pay long-distance telephone charges, find another ISP.

✓ **Do they provide free Internet software?**

Most ISPs provide you with a choice of Netscape Navigator or Internet Explorer free of charge. Make sure that you request that they come in 3.5" floppy disk format if you do not have a CD-ROM player installed in your computer.

✓ **Do they charge for e-mail and how much?**

Some ISPs allow you only a certain number of e-mails per month. If you have many friends and colleagues with e-mail addresses and like to communicate by e-mail, it would be best for you to avoid this type of ISP.

✓ **Do they have subscriptions to newsgroups?**

Some of the larger ISPs are members of thousands of newsgroups, and subscriptions to these newsgroups should be offered free to you.

✓ **Do they service Rockwell 56000 Kbps technology?**

For those of you who would like to use the Rockwell modems, make sure that your ISP can service this new technology.

Before going out and contacting a provider, check with your university. Your university might provide free SLIP/PPP accounts for their students. The university's SLIP/PPP account usually allows you to connect to the Internet for free (less the cost of a local call).

Chapter 2
Navigating The Terrain

Topics

- Structure of the Internet
- Basic Netscape Commands
- Advanced Netscape Controls
- Understanding Frames

This chapter provides a very brief overview of the Internet and one of the main tools for navigating the Internet, Netscape. By now, probably hundreds of books have been written about the Internet, and we cannot possibly hope to cover all topics of interest here. One of the best ways to learn more about the Internet is to check out a free program called *Roadmap 96*, developed by Patrick Crispen. *Roadmap 96* consists of a series of 27 short lessons, each describing some key feature of the Internet. If you already know enough about the Internet to visit a site, you can find *Roadmap 96* at:

http://rs.internic.net/oradmap96/email.html

If you're really a novice, just send an e-mail to listserv@lists.internic.net, and in the body of your message write "Subscribe Roadmaps96 John Doe", substituting your own first and last names for John Doe. Once you send this e-mail, you'll start receiving the 27 lessons on a regular basis over a six- week period. You can work through them at your own pace. In the meantime, let's touch on the basics so you can get started right away.

Structure of the Internet

Before we begin surfing the Internet, let's begin with the basic structure of the Web. The Internet can be viewed as a huge interlocking web of millions of servers around the globe. A helpful analogy might be that the Internet is like the interstate highway system in the U.S. Just as the highway system connects different cities via many different routes, the Internet connects computers around the country and around the world via a number of electronic pathways. That's why the Internet is sometimes described as "a network of networks".

This network of interlocking servers allows users to obtain data and communicate across thousands of miles at a very low cost. Like you and me, hundreds of thousands of others from the far-flung reaches of the globe utilize the Web to research and gather data. Of course, if you want to communicate with a site that is thousands of miles away, you need to know how to find that site. That's where URLs come in. Think of a URL (Universal Resource Locator) as a simple address that identifies the location of any particular point on the Internet. Knowing the URL of a particular site allows you to visit there to see what the site has to offer. A typical URL might look something like this:

www.nyu.edu

There are several components to a URL. The letters in front of the colon simply tell the computer how to access the file or files at the site you want to visit. Most of the sites you're likely to visit will have URLs that begin with http://, but not always. Other possibilities are:

file://
ftp://
telnet://

The second piece of the URL is known as the domain name. In this case, "www" stands for World Wide Web or just "the web". Technically, the Web is just one component of the Internet, though people often refer to the Web and the Internet as if they were the same thing. The rest of the URL, "nyu.edu", indicates that you're looking at a site at New York University (nyu), an educational institution (designated by the characters edu). Some other examples of URLs are:

http://www.cbs.com	Takes you to the web page for the television network, CBS. "com" designates a commercial site.
http://www.akc.org	Takes you to the web page for the American Kennel Club. "org" usually designates some kind of organization other than a business, school or unit of government.
http://www.census.gov	Takes you to the web page for the Bureau of the Census. "gov" indicates a governmental site.

The Internet works in such a way that one site can seamlessly link to another server thousands of miles away. This brings us to the term "hyperlink." Imagine you are reading a page on the Internet and you see a word or words underlined and in blue. This means that if you click this underlined word or phrase, it will link you to another page within the site or anywhere on the Internet. You will understand this better after we have gone over the basic Netscape commands.

Basic Netscape Commands

We are now ready to begin utilizing your Netscape program. Read the instructions from your ISP on how to install Netscape. If you have difficulties, call the support number. When installation is successful, click on the Netscape icon on your screen. Your modem will begin to dial your ISP's telephone number. The first page you will see is your default Home. You can change this default by selecting **Options, Preferences**, described later in this chapter. Below is part of the home page for Netscape (http://home.netscape.com/):

Figure 2.1 Netscape Home Page

The Menu Bar

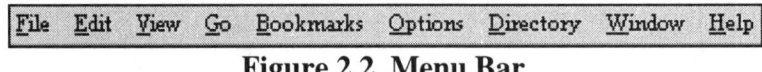

Figure 2.2 Menu Bar

The Menu Bar is like any other in the Windows operating system. Netscape Navigator arranges all the user-accessible features in this manner. *File*, *Edit*, *View*, *Window,* and *Help* are self-explanatory. *Go*, *Bookmarks*, *Options,* and *Directory* are specific to the Internet and will be explained in the next section.

The Tool Bar

Figure 2.3 Netscape Tool Bar

The row of boxes after the Menu Bar is called the Tool Bar. Each of the boxes is an icon or shortcut to commonly utilized commands for surfing the Web. The icons are as follows:

The *Back* Icon

The *Back* icon is used when you need to reverse a step, like an *Undo* button in Windows software. It can be clicked multiple times to go back to whichever site you were previously in.

Lets try the *Back* icon:

> Under the Tool Bar there is an area called "Go to:" Highlight the
> **http://home.netscape.com** blank space and then type in "yahoo" and press "enter."
> Notice that you have hyperlinked to the Yahoo! homepage (description in Chapter 3).
> Now click the *Back* icon. You have returned to the Netscape homepage.

The *Forward* Icon

The *Forward* icon allows you to move one hyperlink forward.

Lets try the *Forward* icon:

> Click on the *Forward* icon. You are now back in the Yahoo! homepage.

The *Home* Icon

The *Home* icon allows you to go to the home address, set as a default in your
Preferences, from wherever you are in the Web. You should use this when you
are lost.

The *Reload* Icon

The *Reload* icon should be utilized if images or pages are not appearing
properly. This icon will download the page again, adjusting images that were
not properly posted on your page.

Lets try the *Reload* button:

> Click on the *Reload* button. The page and all graphics will be reloaded onto your screen.

The *Reload Images* Icon

This icon is shaded because it is currently not active. We will explain this icon in the next section.

The *Open* Icon

Clicking the *Open* icon allows you to input specific addresses on the Internet (commonly called URLs).   This achieves the same objective as highlighting and replacing the statement after *Go To*.

Lets try the *Open* icon:

Click the *Open* icon and a box will appear.
In the white space under the words "Open Location" type **wsj.com** and click on *Open*.

You are in the homepage of *The Wall Street Journal*. With a subscription, you can proceed to enter *The Wall Street Journal Interactive Edition*, to access some of the most complete financial information available on the Web.

The *Print* Icon

Clicking this icon will generate a printout of the current page.

The *Find* Icon

Utilize this icon if you want to search for a specific word in a lengthy document or page.

Lets try the *Find* icon:

Return to the Netscape homepage.
Click the *Find* icon and in the empty space, type "server" and click "OK". You will either get the response "not found" or you will be forwarded to the first "server" word found.

The *Stop* Icon

 The *Stop* icon allows you to stop the download of pages or interrupt the transfer of data from the server to your computer.

Lets try the *Stop* icon:

Click the *Reload* icon and immediately you will notice that the *Stop* icon has turned red. Immediately click the *Stop* icon. You will notice that sections of the page have not been downloaded, particularly the graphics. Click the *Reload* button.

The Directory Bar

The Directory Bar consists of six buttons which, when clicked, link you to Netscape's own list of new, cool, and destination sites.

You are now about ready to start surfing the Internet. Try out the Web and hyperlink to a few sites (refer to Chapter 6 for some interesting sites), and try out all the different icons above.

Advanced Netscape Commands

The *Go* icon in the Menu Bar allows you to visit the sites that you had previously traveled through. This is a handy tool to move more than one hyperlink back, as you will not have to click the *Back* icon multiple times.

The *Bookmark* icon in the Menu Bar is an important tool in expediting your research on the Internet. Clicking this icon allows you to add a bookmark to your favorite or frequently visited sites. Just click on *Bookmark* and Netscape will make a note of the address for you. You can sort your bookmarks by clicking *Go To* and *Bookmark*. You will then be able to create folders in which to keep your favorite bookmarks.
The *Options* button on the Menu Bar, when clicked, enables you to choose the setting for your Netscape Navigator. These options include the following:

General preference. *Change the default setting of your Netscape Navigator browser.* I advise you to carefully consider if you would like to change anything. However, changing the general preference will not seriously impact the running of the program. This option allows you to replace Netscape's default settings. This includes the appearance, fonts, helpers, apps, image quality, and language decryption.

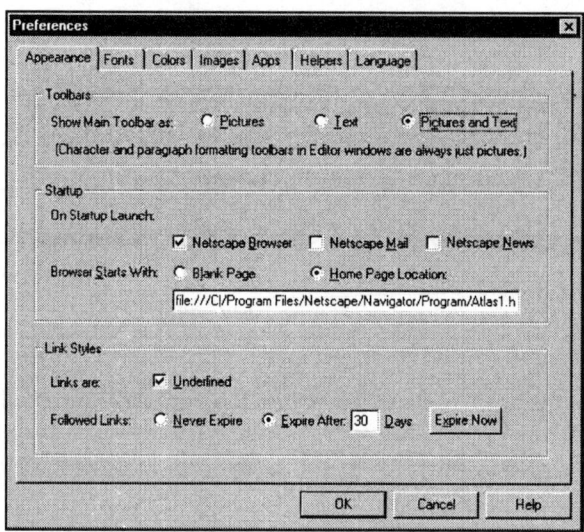

Mail and news preference. *Put your e-mail and news server online.*

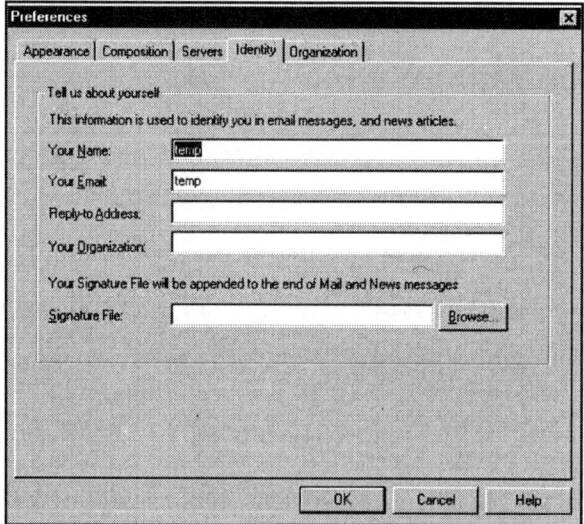

Network preference. *Increase or decrease the size of your cache* (pronounced *cash*) and other network preferences. Cache is an area of memory or file for storing frequently accessed instructions or data. By increasing the memory access time, you may increase the speed of surfing. However, it may slow down the speed of the computer as it will hog more of your RAM. I advise you to look around, but limit the amount of changes that you make here.

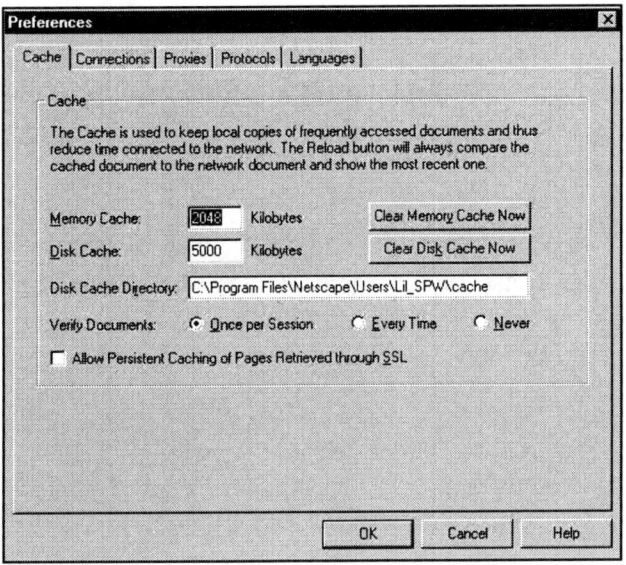

Security preference. This option allows you to create a password for your Netscape browser, and set alert commands and certificates. Utilize this feature when you make a lot of security transactions on the net or are worried other people may use your browser. If you do not trade and utilize automatic logins on the Internet, do not bother with the preferences.

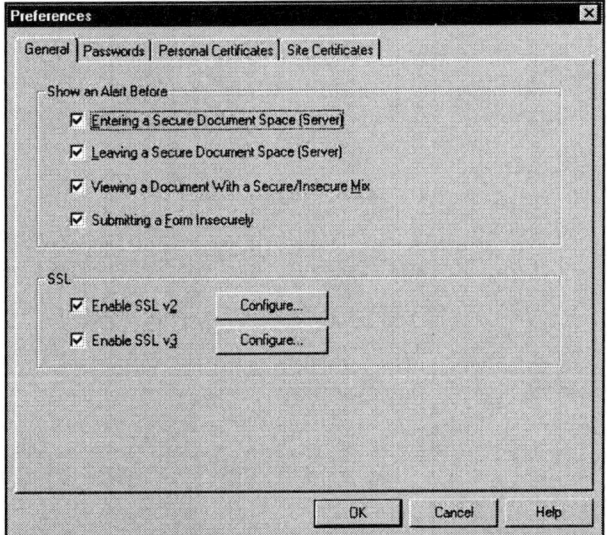

Understanding Frames

Frames are special HTML commands that allow your Netscape Navigator to view more than one HTML document at a time. You can change one pane or window (part of the frame) while freezing the other at the same time. The best way for you to clearly understand this is to take a look at a site with built-in frames. A good example is the New York University site at: **http://www.stern.nyu.edu/students.HTML.**

Notice that the bar on the left is a different HTML file than that on the right. As you hyperlink to another part of the homepage, the left bar will freeze and continually display choices for you to click on.

The above are basic Netscape commands and a few advanced explanations. If you want to know even more about Netscape Navigator, I suggest that you look up the address: **http://home.netscape.com/mozilla/eng/3.0/handbook**. This site will provide more detailed answers to your questions.

Chapter 3
The Search Begins

Topics

- Search Engines
- Yahoo! and other index engines
- AltaVista and other word search engines
- How to find anything, anywhere, and in any language

By now you are an expert surfer and are ready to begin your research on the Web. Before we begin you must understand that the Internet probably contains the largest collection of material in the world. However, unlike the local library that uses the complex Dewey Decimal system to arrange its books in an orderly fashion, the Internet has no particular ordering or easily predictable concentration. If you imagine the Internet as an ocean, the sites are islands created naturally and linked together by a common thread of water, which is the Web. Therefore, to successfully navigate through all these waters and ocean debris, we must be able to utilize a search engine. A search engine is defined as a program on the Internet that lets its user locate online information. There are currently more than 20 available Internet search engines, some specializing in a specific area. Each of these has its own strengths, weaknesses and special features. You should experiment with several of them to determine which works best for your particular needs. These engines are cataloged and updated every day so that data gathered today may not be found tomorrow if they are out of date.

Types of Engines

Now that you have an initial grasp of the concept of the Internet and how to maneuver within it, you must understand the two types of search engines available on the Internet.

Index engines. Index search engines are a collection of engines that allow users to find sites on the Web without actually inputting a search but by following structured categorization. Yahoo!, the result of a classroom experiment of two Stanford students, is widely recognized as the largest and most complete index engine on the Web.

Word engines. A word search engine lets users search its database by inputting keyword combinations and Boolean (explained later in this chapter) additions. This type of search is more complex and may generate a tremendous number of results or "hits." Expert searchers like this type of search engine due to the greater degree of flexibility it allows users and its ability to refine searches. The largest and purest search engine is AltaVista. The line between index engines and word engines becomes gray with sites such as Lycos, which allow for both word and index searches.

Meta engines. These engines let users search multiple databases at the same time. The largest and most well-known meta engine is Metacrawler. This engine allows you to perform basic searches simultaneously in AltaVista, Yahoo!, Lycos, Infoseek, and Webcrawler.

To successfully utilize each search engine, we must first understand how they were designed and their specific rules. These issues are explained below. Descriptions of the various search engines are arranged in order of usefulness to the user, defined as the engine that comes up with the most number of useful "hits" and cross-references to other useful articles. Through simple examples, these descriptions will also alert you to unique rules for the utilization of each search engine. If you need more precise information, consult the help documentation available at each site.

AltaVista Search Engine – http://www.AltaVista.com

AltaVista is the purest and most powerful "word" search engine on the Web. It probably has the largest and most complete indices. However, that does not mean it is the only one you need, nor does it imply that it is the best search engine to use for all research purposes. AltaVista returns consistently useful information, but unfortunately, since no editorial decisions have been made with regard to content, it also has the largest "noise to request" ratio.

AltaVista allows searching of both the Web and many Usenet Newsgroups. It provides both simple and advanced searches and allows the user the choice of viewing search results in standard, compact, or detailed formats. In addition to the features of simple searches, advanced searches allows the user to use Boolean and proximity operators, group terms by parentheses, and rank results by keyword. The site was updated in mid 1997 and currently gives you the option to manually "refine" your search.

Simple Searches

For a successful search using AltaVista, it is best to enter as many search terms or phrases as exactly identify the search topic. The more precise you are or the more exact terms you use, the better the results.

Case sensitivity. Search terms should be entered in lowercase letters to neutralize the case sensitivity of the search engine. The use of capitalized terms (or accented letters) will create a case-sensitive search and will decrease the number of possible hits. Typing the word **BallPoint** finds only the word or phrase exactly in the case typed, whereas typing **ballpoint** will lead you to all occurrences of the word or phrase, regardless of case.

Phrases. To refine your search, you may use quotation marks and group search terms into phrases. For example, **"who is Kurt Kobain?"** finds occurrences of the phrase "who is Kurt Kobain?", capitalized exactly the way you typed.

Forced inclusion. If you want all words that you type to be included in the results, prefix or prepend words with a "**+**" symbol. You would type: **+ballpoint**. Do not leave any space between "**+**" and the word.

Forced exclusion. You may also not want a certain word to appear in search results. To prohibit the inclusion of a word or phrase, prepend it with a "**-**" symbol. To find a reference to Richard Nixon without reference to Watergate, type: **"+Richard Nixon -Watergate"**.

Wildcards. With simple queries you are allowed to enter, at the end of a term or characters, a wildcard character that will substitute for any combination of letters. The asterisk * is AltaVista's wildcard character. For example, typing **immo*** will get all occurrences of immobile, immolate, immoral, immortal, etc. The asterisk cannot be utilized at the beginning or in the middle of words. The asterisk can replace up to 5 additional lower-case letters.

Rankings. AltaVista will assign a confidence ranking to the hits it returns according to the following order:

1. The query terms are found in the first few words of the document (especially in the title of the site).
2. The query terms are found in close proximity to one another in the document.
3. The document contains more of the search terms than other documents.

These factors are weighted, and the document with the highest confidence rating is given a score of 1.00. All others are given decimal scores less than 1.000, in order of their confidence. This does not mean that the highest rated document is the best result found on the topic. It implies only that it best fulfills the criteria of AltaVista's algorithm. Rarely is the "best" source ranked first, unless the topic or search term you typed in is very specific to the site for which you are searching. For example, to find the document "Mr. Carl Sagan's View of the Universe," a search for that phrase, in double quotation marks, will find the exact Web page. But entering the search terms separately, or just searching for "Carl Sagan" will result in too much noise.

Advanced Searches

If doing a simple search does not find you the document you are searching for or it produces too much noise, the advanced search may be your solution. The same rules for capitalization, phrases, wildcards, inclusion/exclusion terms apply to advanced queries. In addition, the use of Boolean searching, proximity operators, and logical groupings with parentheses are allowed. These are only available if you select an advanced search from the AltaVista main page.

Boolean and proximity searching. AltaVista supports the use of the binary operators AND, OR, NEAR and the unary operator NOT. You may enter the operators in lower- or uppercase letters, but it is probably best to use uppercase to make them stand out from ordinary search terms and make the logic of the search more apparent. If these words are part of the terms for which you are searching, they must be enclosed in quotes.

Examples:

- dog AND terrier
- "Richard Nixon" AND "Watergate"
- "Jesse James " AND NOT "gunslinger" (**Note**: Do not use **x NOT y**; it must be **x AND NOT y**)
- "Beavis" OR "MTV"
- TV OR monitor AND "electronics"
- "Carl Sagan" NEAR "solar system"

Results ranking. With advanced searches you may also specify keywords you wish AltaVista to use in order to confidence rank your results. Before submitting your search, type the terms you wish AltaVista to weight more heavily in the Results Ranking Criteria box on the advanced search screen. Then, even though the search results will not be affected, at the top of the listing of hits will probably be those in which you are most interested.

Excite Search Engine - http://www.excite.com

Excite is a hybrid engine that combines word search and subject indices to search either by keyword or by concept. The objective of a concept search is to find documents related to the idea and not just documents containing the search terms. From the home site you will have to choose which way you would like to search by clicking the keyword or concept radio button. You may search reviews, usenet newsgroups, or classifieds on the Web. The simple and advanced search is not separate, as it is in AltaVista. Advanced features like Boolean searching and logical grouping are supported. Unlike Alta Vista, Excite does not allow you to control the appearance of the results, as the engine can utilize only its own default settings.

Case sensitivity. Case sensitivity and words grouped into phrases are not observed in the same way that AltaVista observes them.

Forced inclusion/exclusion. Works in the same way as AltaVista's; prepend a required term with a + symbol and a prohibited term with a - symbol.

Boolean and proximity searching. Excite supports the use of the binary operators AND, OR, and AND NOT and the unary operator NOT. It also supports grouping of terms within parentheses to create complex logic. Booleans and grouping allow for more specific results.

Rankings. The ranking algorithm works as follows: entering a word a greater number of times relative to other words also entered in the search window will ensure that the first documents in the list of results will contain that word. For example, if you type boy boy boy AND girl, Excite will rank the word boy higher than girl in terms of importance, but will find both. Then in the listing of results, documents that contain a greater number of the word "boy" and fewer of the word "girl" will appear at the top of the list. They will be followed by documents that include a greater number of "girl" relative to "boy". Excite also ranks its search results in order of its level of confidence that the document found is a good fit for the search terms entered by the user. The document at the top of the list will not necessarily be 100%.

Search refinement. As you scan the result, look for a document that is very close to the topic you are searching for. Then click the little button next to the confidence rating. This will re-perform the search using search criteria based on the indexing of that particular document, and a new result list will be produced with the document you selected rated 100% and other hits ranked based on their similarity to it.

Infoseek search engine - http://www.infoseek.com

Infoseek was the premiere search engine on the Internet, but it is no longer the best. It has the advantage of both speed and ease of use. Its disadvantage is a lack of sophistication in terms of using both unary and binary operators. Be careful with this engine because you may be charged for searching here. This site is both a search engine and a searchable subject catalog, with options to search Usenet newsgroups, e-mail addresses, and Web FAQs.

Case sensitivity. The engine recognized capitalized words as proper nouns and thereby limits the search. Searching for "Spam" will yield the luncheon meat and Internet advertising. Putting two capitalized word next to each other will turn the query into a phrase. Capitalized phrases must be separated with commas: The Youngest Masters Champion, Top Money Winners. Phrases may also be created by enclosing the words in double quotes just as in AltaVista: "best golf player"; or linking words into phrases by placing hyphens between them: us-open.

Forced inclusion/exclusion. Works the same as AltaVista. Prepend a required term with a + symbol and a prohibited term with a - symbol: +tennis -ball -rackets. Again, there cannot be a space between the symbol and the searched word.

Boolean and proximity searching. Boolean searching is not supported by this engine. Proximity search can be performed by placing words in square brackets. This will cause hits if they are found within 100 words of each other. For example: [vitiligo thyroid]. Check out this site, it may answer the research question you have give up on.

Lycos – http://www.lycos.com

This is one of my favorite search engines. There are better search engines, but Lycos is good and fast, even if it is not as sophisticated as some of the others. It is a hybrid engine that allows both word and index searching (index searches are called directory services). Advantages include speed, ease of use, and sheer size of its indices, which often produces usable results. Disadvantages include the lack of Boolean searching or any of the more sophisticated searches.

Inclusion/exclusion. Lycos does not support the required/prohibited term syntax. Prepending a search term with a - symbol means that that particular term will not be weighted in determining the ranking of the results. For example, planes -Boeing will still yield pages with the word Boeing, but the word Boeing would not be included in the ranking calculation.

Rankings. Lycos ranks each search, rating the best fit as 100% and below. Once again, be careful to accept the 100% as the best match; it merely best fits the search engine's algorithm.

Wildcards. To expand a word with a wildcard, add the $ symbol to the end of the word. For example, type holi$ to get holistic, holiness, holler, etc. Typing the dot or period symbol "." after a word will prohibit its expansion.

Result list/output control. To gain any sort of control over your searches in Lycos, you need to click on the *Enhance your Search* link on the Lycos front page. You will be taken to a screen that will allow you to control the following:

- The type of match between search terms
- The content of the hits
- The number of documents per page (for example, 10, 20, 30, or 40)
- The type of match for terms (loose, fair, good, close, strong)

Tip: You can refine the results of your searches by changing the type of matches Lycos considers a success: loose, fair, good, close, and strong. The strong option will yield fewer hits, but they will be better hits. This engine will also reject broad words that will generate more than 1000 hits. Anyway, who would look at more than 100 hits?

Webcrawler – http://www.webcrawler.com

Webcrawler is an outstanding search engine very similar to AltaVista. It has more power than AltaVista in implementing advanced search features such as the proximity operators. Like Excite and Lycos, this site is also a hybrid engine that has both a powerful search engine and large indexing capabilities. It implements a feature of further searching based on pre-set search terms from the subject catalog, very much like Excite.

Result/output control. On the initial search screen you can choose the *Option* button. This will allow you to choose whether you want to see Web titles only or titles and summaries for each document. You may also select the number of hits per page, for example 10, 25, or 100. The summary option will display a brief abstract of each page, its address, and its confidence ranking. I advise you to use the title option, which will increase your reading speed. In addition, there is an icon under the "search results" that will allow you to toggle between summary and title option.

Confidence rankings. Next to each hit a percentage is displayed. The closer the percentage is to 100%, the higher the confidence match between the page and the search term. You will also see a numeric version of the confidence ranking when the summary option is chosen. The confidence rankings seem to be no more than a count of the occurrences of the search term within a particular document.

Phrases. As with AltaVista, if you want terms to be considered a phrase, you may enter them in double quotes. This means that words must appear next to each other in the yielded document. If combined with an additional term, this will yield better results on the first try, for example King AND "I have a dream".

Boolean and proximity searching. Excite supports the use of the binary operators AND, OR, and AND NOT and the unary operator NOT. It also supports grouping of terms within parentheses to create complex logic. Booleans and grouping allow for more specific results. Webcrawler's most advanced features lie in the implementation of its proximity operators. You may utilize NEAR/x, where x is the number of words apart the two search words should be. For example Lennon NEAR/3 music. If the x is not specified, the NEAR operator will yield documents where the words are next to each other, in any order. For specific order control you must utilize the ADJ operator: Pentium ADJ computers. In this example, the word *Pentium* must precede *computer*.

Inclusion/exclusion. Not supported.

Wildcards. Not supported.

Site plus: shortcuts. The *Shorcut* icon is used to increase ease of use for the searcher. *Shortcut* allow you to do the following:

- Add a city name to your search; get shortcuts to maps and weather for that city.
- Search for a stock ticker symbol; get a shortcut to the latest stock price.
- Search for your favorite musical artist; get shortcuts to their albums in the online music store.
- Search for the car you are looking for; get a shortcut to free classified listings.
- Search for the computer you want to buy; get a shortcut to classifieds listings.

Webcrawler excels in ease of use and complex proximity search features, but its indices seem to be smaller than those of AltaVista or Lycos. In addition, the site has some interesting features such as "search the web backwards" which enables you to see who is linked to your page, Internet statistics, and shortcuts.

Yahoo!- http://www.yahoo.com

Yahoo! is the premiere index engine on the Web today. Yahoo! is strictly hierarchically arranged and has been developed over a long period of time, with a lot of editorial care. Yahoo! is the best tool for searching for good or general sites when you are not certain (or are less concerned) about what results you want to achieve. It is a good place to find the search word that can then be utilized to do more advanced searches. Starting in early 1997, Yahoo! collaborated with the AltaVista search engine to allow a seamless transfer from one engine to another. This means that a search in Yahoo! may automatically be re-performed in AltaVista. In combination, this site is one of the most powerful search location on the Web. It is a perfect marriage of two different search engines.

Searching with Yahoo! is very simple. You may just enter your search term(s) in the search window and click *Search*. Yahoo! will return three types of information:

1. Yahoo! categories that match the search term (so you can explore them for cross referencing).
2. Actual matching end-sites.
3. Yahoo! categories from which the various pages are indexed like a "much broader term" cross-reference.

You are limited in the complexity of the searches, but you may still control display and output control, which may be accessed by clicking the small "options" link next to the main search window. Within this feature, you can control the following:

Where to search. Yahoo! (default), Usenet or e-mail addresses

Search method. OR or AND (default) search terms are utilized whether to search on substrings (for example, if you want to find whole words from partial strings -- like "headlines" when searching for the word "head") or complete words (find "headlines" only when entering the term "headlines"). The substring option is the default for this search engine.

Search area. You have the option to choose just Yahoo! or both Yahoo! and AltaVista.

Listing date. You have the option to find new items only.

Results per page. You can choose to have 10, 22 (default), 50 or 100 results listed on each page.

Yahoo! has a couple of other unique features. At the bottom of each results page, links to search engines are provided. By clicking on *Yahoo Remote*, you can invoke a secondary Netscape window, which you can minimize and then maximize whenever you need to do a quick search. If the essential search engine is AltaVista, the essential subject catalog is Yahoo!. Together, they have become one of the most prominent search engines on the Web.

Summary of Engines

Search Engines	Case Sensitive	Phrases	Forced Inclusion	Forced Exclusion	Wild-card	Results Ranking?	Bool-eans	Proximity Operators	Indexing	Refine
AltaVista	Y	Y	+	-	*	Y	Y	Y	N	Y
Excite	N	N	+	-	N	Y	Y	N	Y	Y
WebCrawler	N	Y	N	N	N	Y	Y	Y	Y	N
Lycos	N	N	N	N	$	Y	N	N	Y	N
InfoSeek	Y	Y	+	-	N	Y	N	Y	Y	N
Yahoo!	N	N	N	N	N	N	N	N	Y	N

How to Save Your Findings

After all your hard work and sleuthing, you have found the article or articles that you may be interested in, without reading them completely. Leave the reading for later, speed is of the essence and there is cost to your being on-line.

Option 1: Save the file in .txt (text) form:

1. Click the "file" in your menu bar

2. Choose "save as"

3. Change "save as type" to ".txt" (look in the bottom of the box; there should be a down arrow; click on it)

4. Type: **a:filename.txt** (limit file name to an 8 letter or number combination)

This will allow you to open the file in Word later. (**Hint**: do not try this with tables; it will really get messy.) If the file looks messy, try changing the font to Courier 10; it usually works.

Option 2: Cut & paste into Word – expert Windows users only

1. Open a word processing program.

2. Highlight the area or article that you are interested in and press Ctrl-C.

3. Press Alt-tab to go back into Word and paste into the document. (**Hint**: do not try this with tables; it will really get messy.)

Option 3: Print

This option can be costly; however, it is a necessary evil when tables or graphics are involved.

Choose your option wisely. It would not be a great idea to print everything unless you are in a terrible hurry. Printing also takes time and may slow down your search.

Trouble Shooting Searches

Too Many Results

- Be more specific describing the topic.
- Use more keywords and relate them with logical AND.
- Require the presence of the most relevant words.
- Delete similar words of no interest using logical NOT.
- Use, if possible, phrases instead of single words..
- Constrain the search to concrete fields . For example: Title, Specific Urls, link name, or host name.
- Use capital letters for names and use accents.
- Write the word in any language other than English.
- If you want to give more importance to a certain word, simply repeat it.

No or Few Results

- Delete keywords leaving only the most relevant ones.
- Change AND by logical OR .
- Check your spelling, especially if you should have gotten more results.
- Use synonyms and variants.
- Change or include the other grammatical number. For example: book to books; pencil to pencils.
- Write everything in lowercase letters.

- Use more universal searchers, and use English.
- It is always possible that there isn't much information about your topic.

The Search is Too Slow

- Delete common or frequently used words. Don't use words with few syllables, like articles, which will not facilitate the search and will prolong the search unnecessarily.
- Do not use a lot of words. Delete the superfluous ones.
- Change to another searcher; it might be overloaded. Or make the search in another moment.
- Deactivate automatic loading of graphics until you get an interesting objective.
- If you want to go to a noncontiguous page, use the menu option GO.

Search Tips & Tricks

1. Start with the appropriate or good search engine.
2. Narrow your search mentally before typing your request.
3. Try the obvious; if you are looking for a specific question, use quote marks: "what is dyslexia?"
4. Be careful of your spelling.
5. Don't fear the Boolean.
6. Play by the rules of the search engines being utilized.
7. Not all search engines are created equal.
8. If you find something, bookmark it for bibliography purposes.

Chapter 4
The Wall Street Journal
Interactive Edition

One of the best resources for financial information on the Internet is *The Wall Street Journal® Interactive Edition.* This site contains a wealth of current and archival financial news, company information, stock quotes, and other financial and statistical information. Need to research a company for a class project? This is a great place to start. Want to create and track a portfolio of stocks and/or mutual funds? You can do that here, too. Looking for advice on how to invest your money wisely? Look no further.

If you are familiar with the print version of *The Wall Street Journal®*, you'll find navigating around the *Interactive Journal* site a snap. The site is organized by section, just like the print version. The front section contains the major business and news stories of the day, news summaries, columns on sports and the arts, and the editorial pages. Marketplace–Section B in the print version–offers articles and columns that often have an industry-specific focus like technology, law or small business. Money and Investing® (Section C of the print version) contains the kind of information for which *The Wall Street Journal* is famous: articles about the latest movements in the financial markets, statistical information on closely-watched barometers like the Dow Jones Industrial Average or the Standard & Poors 500, the well-known column *Heard on the Street®*, and more.

Of course, the *Interactive Journal* is much more than an electronic version of the newspaper. In Marketplace, for example, you can join discussion groups to talk about the latest ups and downs of the Dow, Microsoft's latest antitrust battles, and a host of other hot topics. In Money and Investing, you can enter ticker symbols for stocks or mutual funds to check their current prices. The *Interactive Journal* also has a Personal Journal® section that you can customize to suit your interests. The site allows you to create folders to collect news articles on particular topics or companies. You can also construct as many as 5 different portfolios, each containing up to 30 stocks or mutual funds, and track these portfolios on a daily basis.

The most valuable feature is that the *Interactive Journal* permits users to do their own, in-depth research on individual companies or broader topics covered in the financial press. You can search for and retrieve all articles about a given company, product, or subject over periods ranging from the most recent two weeks to the last two years. If you don't want to sift through a collection of articles, the site provides more focused Briefing Books. A typical Briefing Book includes quantitative and qualitative information about publicly-traded companies, s descriptive history of the company, recent news articles or press releases, current and historical stock price and trading volume data, and financial statement information like revenues and earnings per share. To retrieve this information you simply point to the appropriate area on the site and enter the company's name or stock ticker symbol.

Let's take a closer look at the site to see what you'll find when you visit it. After a quick overview of the types of information available, we'll illustrate how to use the site to research a particular topic or company.

Site Layout

When you point your browser to the URL http://wsj.com, you'll see *The Wall Street Journal Interactive Edition* banner across the top of the screen, with three columns of text underneath. (Note: This site is continually being updated, and the layout is subject to change. The column on the far left contains information about subscribing to or advertising on the site. The column in the middle contains a few of the biggest headlines of the day. You will be interested in the column on the right, which allows you to follow links to just about any part of the site. A logical place to start is the Front Page, so be sure that text is highlighted in the box and click "Go". (Keep in mind that this is a subscription-based site, and access to most of this site is limited to subscribers.)

The Front Page section is organized with the banner across the top and three columns of text underneath, also. The column on the left contains links to other parts of the site.

From this column you can follow links directly to the Money and Investing section or any other part of the *Journal* that you want to explore. The middle column contains the *Journal's* familiar news summaries with links to take you to the full text of featured articles. The third column offers a mix of news stories, links to other parts of the site, and near the bottom, access to the site's search capabilities and briefing books.

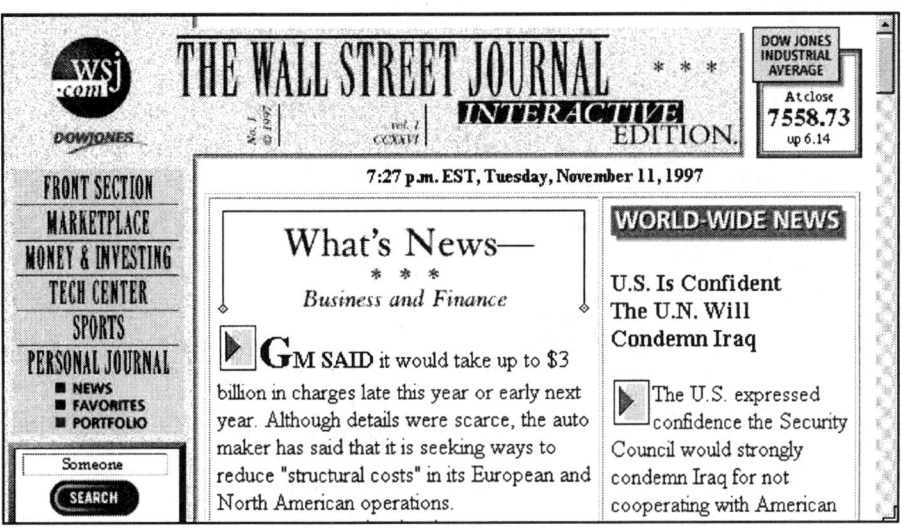

Point to the left-hand column and click on the Money and Investing link. Essentially this section follows the same three-column layout described above, but with a few twists. Many people will want to bookmark this page because right at the top it provides a graph that plots that day's value of the Dow at 5-minute intervals. If you check this graph consistently over time, you'll notice that the Dow is most volatile at the beginning and at the end of the trading day. If you spend a lot of time going back and forth between different sections of the site, be sure to hit your "Reload" button when you revisit this page or any other area that contains updated financial data.

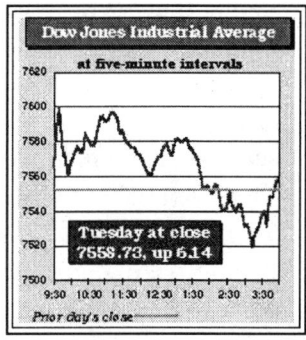

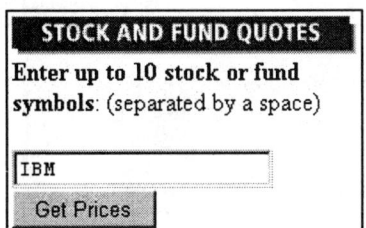

Scroll down to the bottom of the Money & Investing page, and on the right you'll find a box where you can enter ticker symbols for stocks or mutual funds. Enter a symbol or a group of symbols and you'll receive the latest price quote and trading volume figures for the stocks you selected (delayed 20 minutes). Try out this feature by entering IBM and clicking *Get Prices*. Look at the output provided then click the Back button on your browser to return to Money & Investing.

Suppose you know what topic you want to explore, but you don't know where on the site you're most likely to find information related to that topic. A convenient way to search the site for broad topic areas is to check out the Table of Contents. A link to this area can be found in the left column, about halfway down the page. Click the link, and you'll see a comprehensive outline of just about everything the site has to offer. Click on any part of the outline for a link to that particular area. (**Note:** The structure of the Table of Contents is much like the index search engine Yahoo that we described in Chapter 3.)

In general, the best way to become acquainted with what's available in the *Interactive Journal* is to spend time exploring it on your own. Rather than going step-by-step over every single part of the site, let's turn our attention to using the site to do research, to learn more about any given topic or company. It is the research capabilities of the *Interactive Edition* that will be of most use to students.

THE WALL STREET JOURNAL INTERACTIVE EDITION — **TABLE OF CONTENTS**

Personal Journal | Portfolio | Search | Briefing Books | Journal Links

FRONT SECTION
- Front Page
- World-Wide
- Asia
- Europe
- The Americas
- Economy
- Earnings Focus
- Politics & Policy

Opinion
- Editorial Page
- Leisure & Arts
- Voices

Leisure & Arts Resource Center
- Book Reviews
- Film Reviews
- Theater Reviews

TECH CENTER
- Tech Main Page
- Systems
- Ventures
- Fast Forward
- Tech Stocks

Recent Special Reports
- Health and Medicine
- Asian Economic Survey
- Retirement

Weather
- United States
- Asia
- Europe

Feature of the Week

WSJ.COM Radio lets you tune in the top business and markets news, updated hourly between 10 a.m. and 4 p.m. EST weekdays.

Other news about wsj.com

MARKETPLACE
- Marketplace page
- Business Focus
- Health & Science
- Law
- Marketing & Media
- Small Business Suite
- Who's News

Marketplace columns
- Health Journal (M)
- Managing Your Career (T)
- Work & Family (W)
- Personal Technology (Th)
- The Front Lines (F)

Weekly features
- Property Report (W)
- Home Front (F)
- Travel (F)

Regional Journals
- California
- Florida
- New England
- Southeast
- Texas

SPORTS
- Sports Front Page

BARRON'S ONLINE
- This Week's Barron's
- Weekday Extra
- Market Lab
- Archives / Search

SMARTMONEY INTERACTIVE
- Main Page
- Best Buys
- Broker Ratings
- Pundit Watch

CAREERS.WSJ.COM

Careers.wsj.com is the Web's premier site for career-related news and information, as well as thousands of searchable listings of management and professional positions.

MONEY & INVESTING
- Money & Investing page
- Data Bank
- Markets Data Center
- U.S. Stocks
- Small U.S. Stocks
- Heard on the Street
- Americas Stocks
  - Argentina
  - Brazil
  - Canada
  - Mexico
- Asia Stocks
  - Heard in Asia
  - Australia
  - Hong Kong
  - Indonesia
  - Japan
  - Malaysia
  - Philippines
  - Singapore
  - South Korea
  - Taiwan
  - Thailand
- Europe Stocks
  - Heard in Europe
  - Belgium
  - Britain
  - France
  - Germany
  - Italy
  - The Netherlands
  - Spain
  - Sweden
  - Switzerland
- South African Stocks
- Credit Markets
- Foreign Exchange
- Commodities
- Mutual Funds
- Personal Finance Center
- Earnings Surprises
- Insider Trading Spotlight

Resources
- The Getting Going Center
- BanxQuote Banking Center
- Glossary
- Mutual Fund Scorecards
- Zacks Investment Research

Calendars
- U.S. Economic Calendar
- Int'l Economic Calendar
- Securities Offering Cal.
- Economic Indicators
- Earnings Calendar

Customer Service: Help | Contact Us | Your Account

Advertising: Advertisers | E-Mart: Classified Ads

Return to top of page

Copyright © 1997 Dow Jones & Company, Inc. All Rights Reserved.

Research Capabilities

Briefing Books

A Briefing Book is a collection of information about a particular company. When you want to learn more about a specific company, looking at the company's Briefing Book may be the best way to begin. You can find hyperlinks to the Briefing Book section no matter where you are on the site. Most often the link to Briefing Books will be located in the column on the far left of the screen. Less commonly it will appear at the top or bottom of a particular page. Find one of these links and click it.

When you search for a Briefing Book on a given company, you must enter either the company name or the stock ticker symbol. If you know it, the stock ticker symbol is usually the best choice because different firms often have very similar names. If you don't know the ticker symbol, just enter the full name of the firm. Sometimes you may be presented with a menu of firms with similar names before retrieving a briefing book, so be sure you know which firm you really want.

Let's say you want to learn more about The Finish Line, an athletic footwear and apparel retailer. Once you are in the Briefing Books section, type the ticker symbol FINL in the box provided, then click *Get Briefing Book*. The next screen offers several choices for additional information:

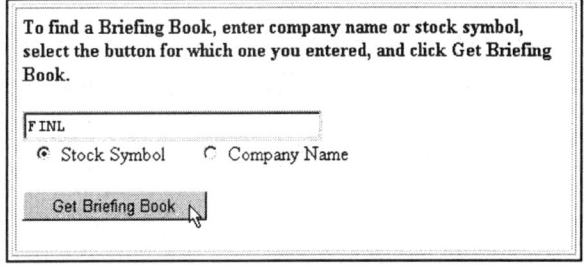

Company Background. - a brief text description of the nature of the company's business, the firm's address, a list of key officers, and some recent financial data.

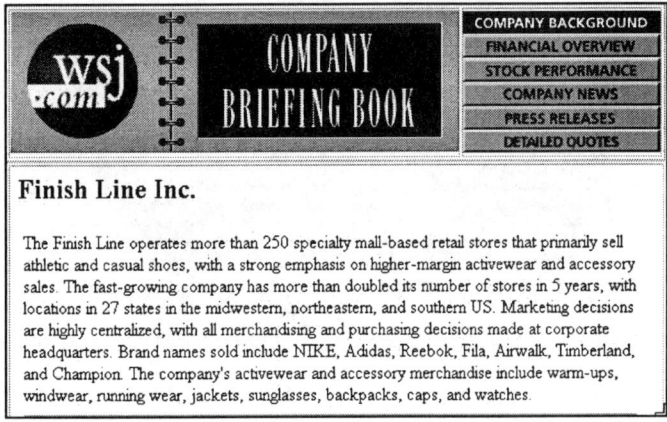

Financial Overview. - quarterly and annual information such as earnings per share, revenues, income, assets, and recent values of selected financial ratios.

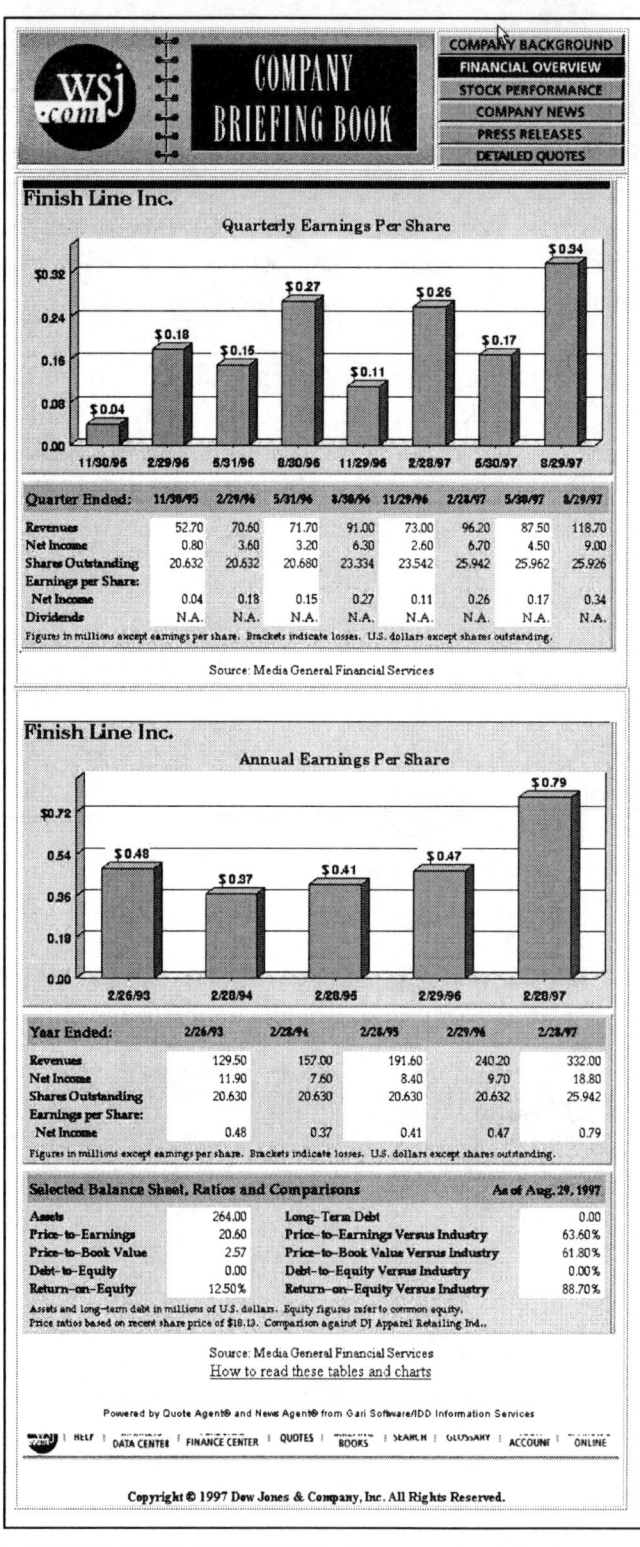

Stock Performance. - recent and historical stock price, return and trading volume data presented in tabular and graphical form.

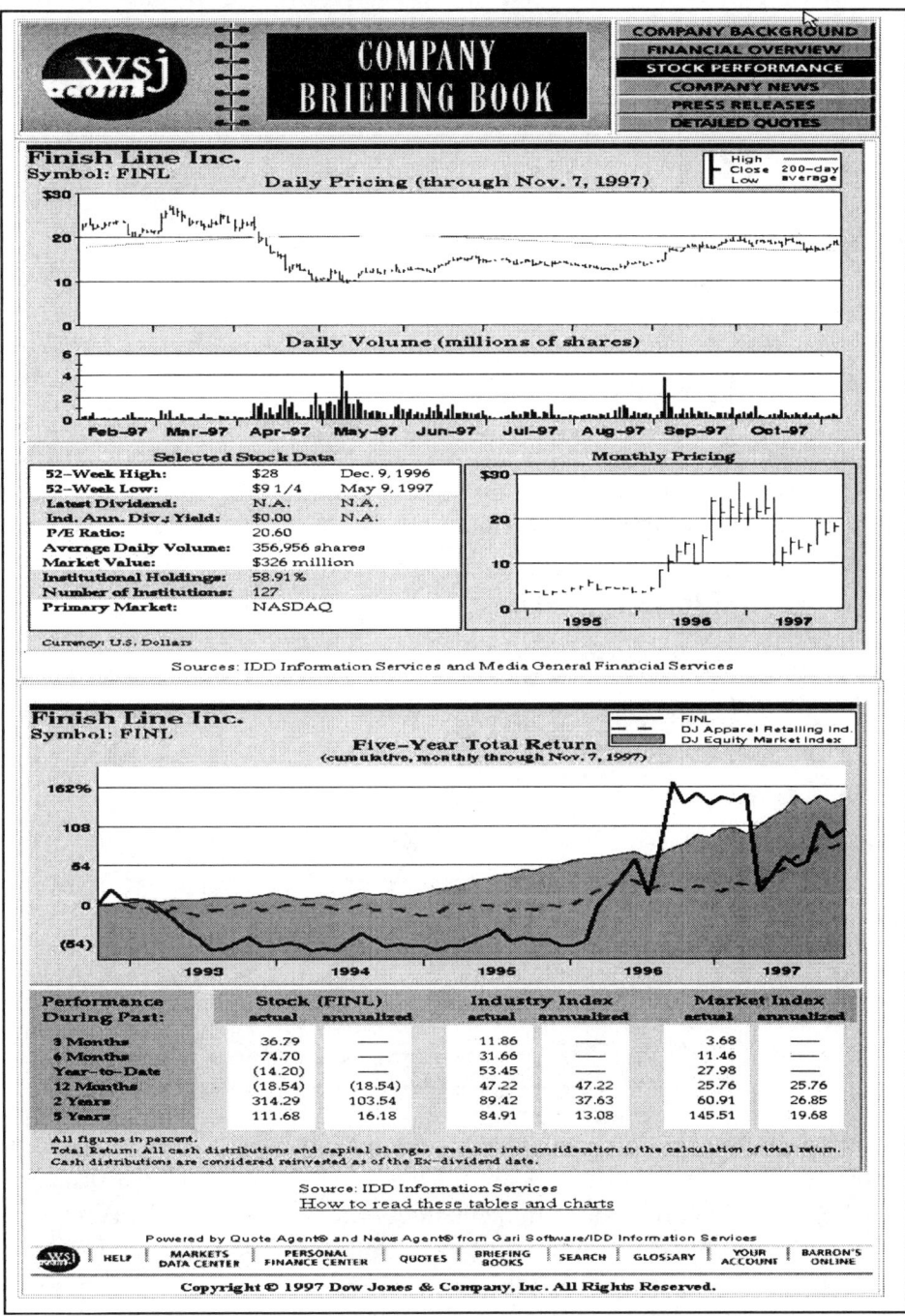

Company News. - articles that have appeared in the *Journal* or the Dow Jones Newswires over the previous two weeks.

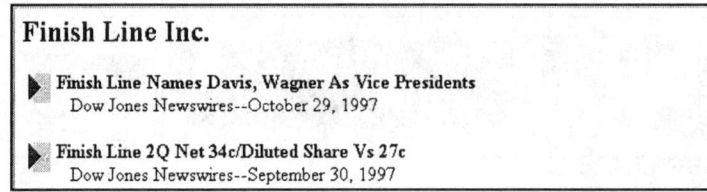

Press Releases. - recent information released by the company.

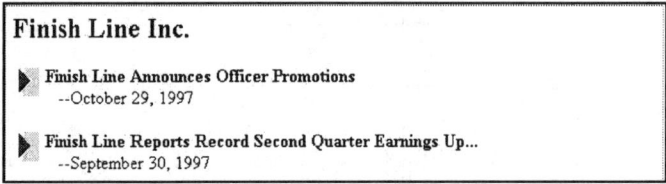

Detailed Quotes. - current data on the stock price and trading volume (delayed 20 minutes), including daily high and low figures and 52-week high and low quotes.

Finish Line Inc.

Symbol: FINL

COMPOSITE TRADING		Prices Delayed 20 Minutes	
November 11		November 10	
Last:	17 5/8	Close:	17 7/8
Change:	- 1/4	Change:	- 1/4
Volume:	80,300	Volume:	54,900
Time:	4:45 p.m. ET		
Exchange:	Nasdaq		
Day Open:	17 7/8		
Day High:	18	52-Week High:	28
Day Low:	17 5/8	52-Week Low:	9 1/4

Clearly you can learn a lot about a company simply by browsing through its Briefing Book. You can plot sales trends, compare the company's stock price performance to a broader index, monitor current developments involving or affecting the company, and obtain an address to write the firm directly for more information. You might want to select several Briefing Books to make direct comparisons between companies that compete in the same line of business. If you want to capture some of this data for later analysis, be sure to print out the relevant pages.

Two other areas of the Briefing Books reports are worth mentioning. At the bottom of the initial Briefing Books screen you'll find links to other sites providing more information about the firm. The EDGAR site maintained by the Securities and Exchange Commission is one of the best sources on the web for financial information.

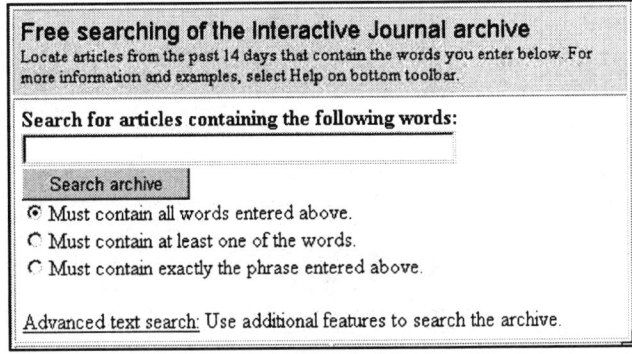

Securities laws require firms to file all kinds of periodic reports, and EDGAR makes these reports available to you. You can find more detailed financial information here, as well as data on who owns large positions of stock in the company, insider trading, and lots of other goodies. The other interesting link is to Zacks, a source that compiles analysts' reports and summarizes their recommendations in convenient ways. For example, you can see how many analysts recommend that investors buy or sell a given stock. Zacks also reports forecasts for the firm's earnings per share.

Searching News Archives

Another powerful research tool available at this site is the search facility that allows you to comb through articles from the *Journal* or the Dow Jones Newswires. You can focus your search on just the most recent two days, two weeks, or the past two years. You can also look for articles written by a particular person.

To try out the search facility, look for the "Search" link. Like the link for Briefing Books, you'll usually find the search link in the left-hand column. Click on the search link. The *Interactive Journal* allows both simple and advanced search strategies. When you click on the search link, you are first offered the opportunity to conduct a very basic search. You do not have the option to use Boolean operators that we covered in an earlier chapter. Instead, the *Interactive Journal* asks you to enter the text that you want to search for and then to select from a menu of search options that are similar to Boolean logic. Your choices are:

- Must contain all words entered above (similar to Boolean operator AND)
- Must contain at least one of the words (similar to Boolean operator OR)
- Must contain exactly the phrase entered above.

At first you should experiment with the different options to better understand the results you are likely to obtain with each. As is always the case in these kinds of searches, you face the tradeoff of more precision (i.e., finding articles that cover exactly what you're looking for) versus more quantity (i.e., finding lots of articles that are related in some way to your topic). Notice that this tool provides another way to locate articles about specific companies. Rather than going to the news portion of a firm's Briefing Book, you can go straight to the search area and type in the company name.

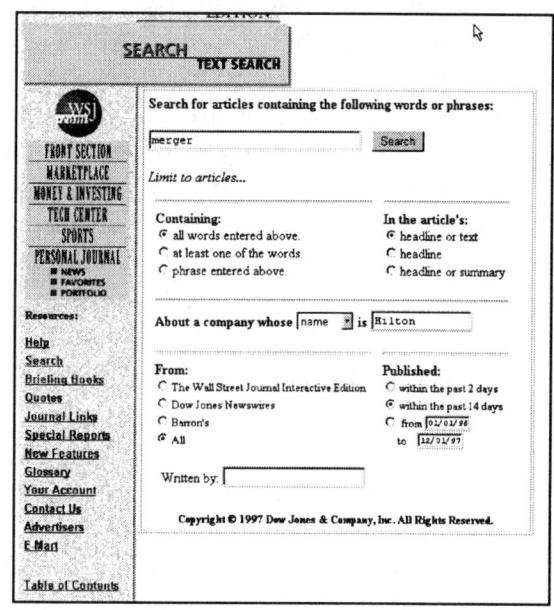

At times you may want to conduct more complex search strategies. Just under the menu of options related to the text you enter in the search box, you'll see a link called "Advanced text search." Click it.

In this area you have the same options you had before plus a lot more. For example, you can look for specific words that appear only in the headline of an article. You can look for articles that appeared more than two weeks ago. You can look for articles that appeared in the *Interactive Journal*, the Dow Jones Newswires, Barron's, or all three sources. You can combine a topical search with a company search (e.g., type "merger" in the first search box and then type "Hilton" in the company name box).

Once you get a list of articles, you may see the entire article by clicking the black box that appears just before the headline text. This box also indicates the source of the article. If your search yields too many articles, you can click the *Refine Your Search* button, which takes you back to the advanced search menus.

Premium Search Feature

You can also expand the universe of your search by using the Dow Jones Publications Library. Covering over 3,700 publications, including most major newspapers and business periodicals, it's like having a library at your fingertips. Searching is always free, and you get the first three lines of the articles to review. Additional charges will apply should you wish to view the entire article.

To access the Publications Library, click on those words on the main page. The screen below indicates the range of searching capabilities at this site.

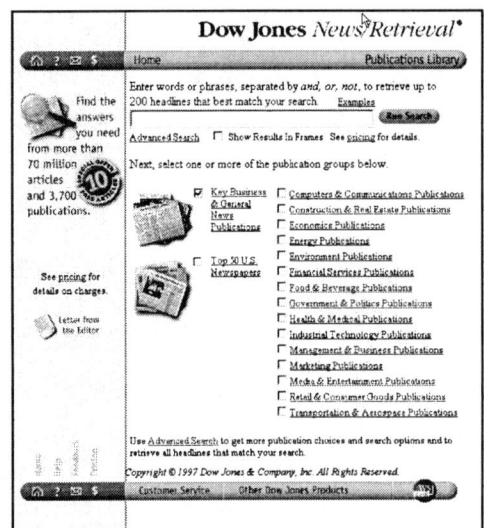

Other Tools

Though the Briefing Books and search engine are probably the best tools for doing research on the *Interactive Journal*, there is a great deal more for the enterprising student to experiment. Here is a brief summary of some of the other interesting parts of this site.

Personal Journal

In this section you can create folders containing news stories about companies or topics that you select. This is a useful way to organize the research that you have done, and allows you to follow news stories of interest over time. To create a folder, just click one of the *Edit* buttons and you will be prompted for additional information to define the contents of your folder.

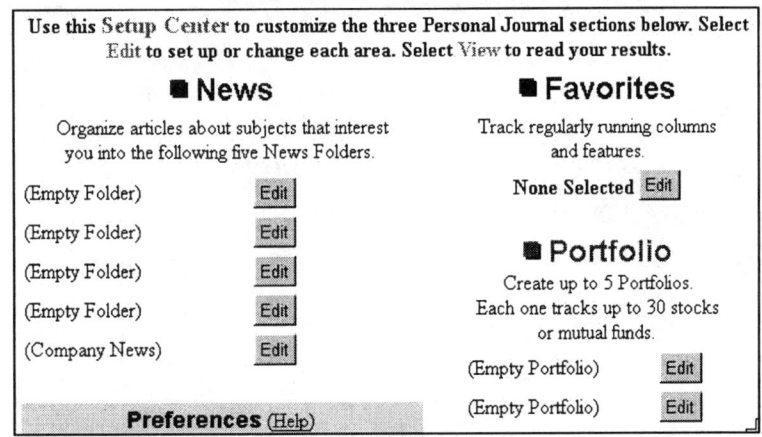

You can also create and track portfolios of stock or mutual funds. Just click an *Edit* button and you'll be asked to identify the stocks in your portfolio, the number of shares, the purchase price, and the purchase date. You might

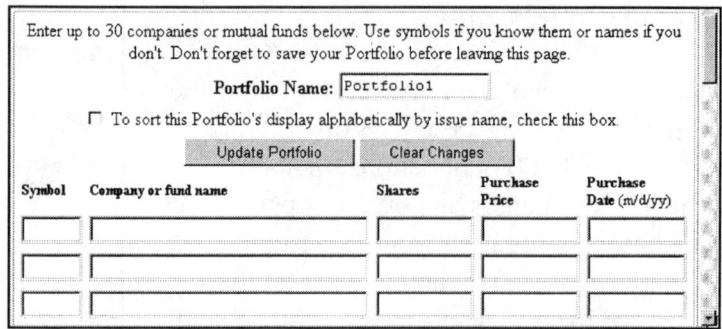

create 5 portfolios with each being concentrated in a particular industry. Or your portfolios might consist of mutual funds, with each portfolio containing funds of a particular type (e.g., stock funds, bond funds, growth funds, international funds).

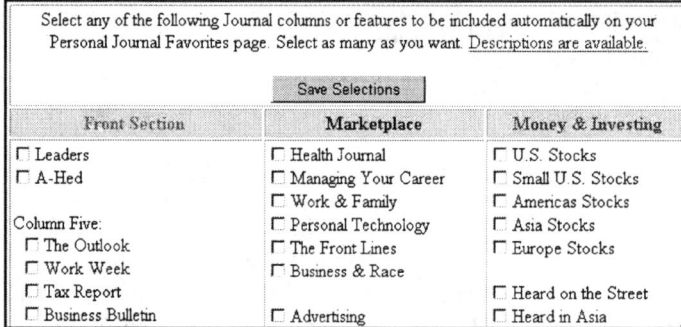

Finally, Personal Journal lets you identify your favorite sections of the *Interactive Journal* and keep track of those on a regular basis. For example, you might want to save the Personal Technology and Heard on the Street columns whenever they appear.

Just configure your "Favorites" accordingly and the *Interactive Journal* will do the rest.

Voices

Voices is an interactive discussion group where you can share your opinions on the latest issues affecting business, the marketplace, or technology with other subscribers. The topics available here will change from time to time. Like other discussion groups around the web, this is a good place to hear what other people are thinking about the latest issues.

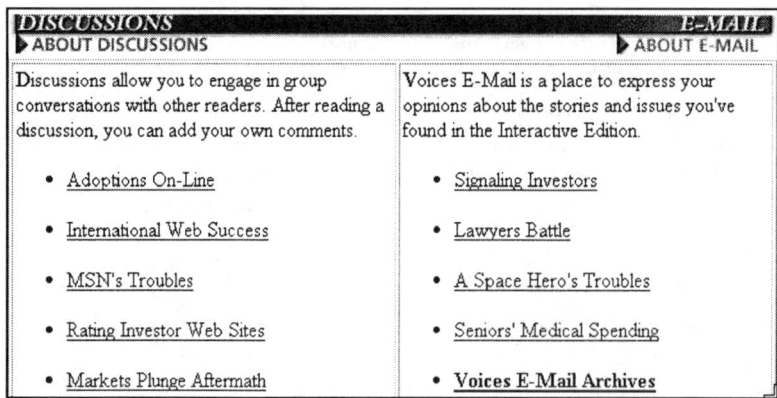

Money & Investing

This section, described briefly at the beginning of the chapter, contains more links to financial data than any other does. Just about anything that you can find in the printed version of the Journal you can find here, everything from domestic and international stock markets, to bonds, to mutual funds, to commodities. There is also a link here to the Personal Finance Center and to Personal Finance Tools, two areas focused on helping individuals manage their own money more effectively. The breadth of information in this area can be a little overwhelming. Take time to explore it.

In this Section:
Data Bank
Markets Data Center
U.S. Stocks
Small Stocks
Technology Stocks
Americas Stocks
Asia Stocks
Europe Stocks
Heard on the Street
Credit Markets
Foreign Exchange
Commodities
Mutual Fund News
Mutual Fund Data
Personal Finance Center
Personal Finance Tools

Useful Links

In the Briefing Books section we mentioned the links to the SEC EDGAR site and to Zacks. There are a number of links to additional interesting sites, as seen below:

Related Sites:
Barron's Online
SmartMoney Interactive
Careers.wsj.com
Business Directory
Publications Library

Some of these sites reside on the *Interactive Edition*, and some outside. Access to some is free, while others are available exclusively to *Interactive Edition* subscribers.

Additional interesting links can be found in Chapter 6 of this book.

Summary

The *Interactive Journal* is an invaluable research tool for students who need to know more about companies or business issues. The site allows you to look at the most recent news and information about a company, or information going several years back. There is quantitative and qualitative material to examine and synthesize. If the information you are looking for is not here, there is probably a link to take you to what you need.

Chapter 5
Creating A Home to Call Your Own

Topics

- What Is HTML?
- What are the HTML codes and how do they work?
- How do I create my own Web page?

What is HTML?

HTML stands for Hypertext Markup Language, a programming language that allows Web pages to be read by browsers in multi-platforms. This language allows the programmer to insert video and audio, and also enables the programmer to hyperlink to other documents on the Internet. HTML has become the standard on the Internet.

What Are the HTML Codes and How Do They Work?

At first glance, the HTML language looks terrifying and extremely complicated. However, it is actually simpler than it looks. HTML works somewhat like an old typewriter. The typewriter must be told to start and end the boldfacing or underlining of certain words and phrases in a document. As with a typewriter, you must instruct the browser to do the same for your Web page. These instructions come in the form of Tags. Tags are instructions to the browser on how to format a document, such as line breaks, paragraph breaks, or italics. A command in HTML always begins with **\<tag\>** and ends with **\</tag\>**. For example, if you want to bold the word "hello" in HTML, you must sandwich "hello" in the instructions for bold, as follows: **\<B\>Hello\</B\>**. Tags are not case sensitive, but they are highly sensitive to spelling errors. There are a large number of HTML Tags. Take a look at the list of Tags in Appendix 5.1 and try to understand what each tag means.

How to Create Your Own Simple Web Pages

Before you begin with your own home building exercise, you should create sketches, or mentally picture how you want your Web pages to look like. Use your imagination; there is little that cannot be done on the Web, and this includes audio and video. However, bear in mind that a Web site not only has to look good, it must also function and serve the user well. By now, you will have noticed that some sites on the Web are very logically designed while others seem more haphazard, as if they were the creation of several different people. Therefore, it is important to design a well-organized site.

A simple structure may look as follows:

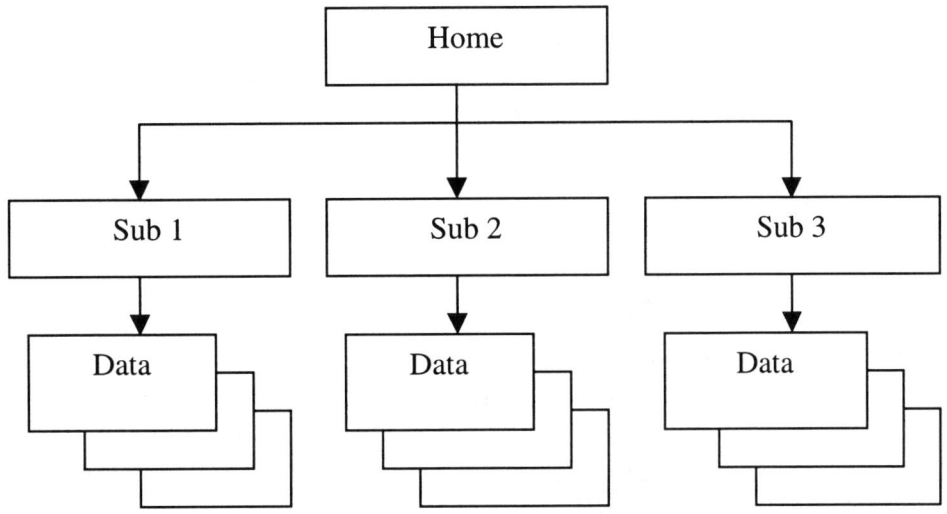

Level 1: The home page, the index that allows the user to go directly to any and all other pages on your site.

Level 2: A subdirectory to the original index/home page.

Level 3: The data or stories you want the public to access.

You also should not forget to link back to the home page or subdirectory. Once you have completed the sketches, you are ready to design your home page. But like a chef in the kitchen, you must first gather the ingredients. In this case, the ingredients are the images and background. To view images or backgrounds that appeal to you, visit the sites below.

These sites contain good texture, images, or backgrounds.

The Graphic Station	http://www.geocities.com/SiliconValley/6603/
Texture Land	http://www.meat.com/textures/
HTML Goodies	http://www.htmlgoodies.com/

Once you have found a picture or background that you like, bring the cursor to the image. Click on the right button of the mouse and a table will appear.

1. Insert a floppy disk in your **A** drive.

2. Choose *save **image as***

3. Type **a:image1** in the white area under the words *File Name*.

4. Take note of the type of image that is being downloaded by looking under *Files Save As Type* and click *OK*. You have just downloaded the image into your floppy drive.

Be careful of copyrights and logo restrictions and make sure you read their FAQ or agreement pages.

There are two standard graphic formats or extensions on the Internet. They are the *.gif* and the *.jpg*. If you would like to see the image that you have saved, click on the *Open* icon and type **a:image1.jpg**. If nothing shows up, try **a:image1.gif**.

Now that you have gathered the ingredients, it is time to prepare the cooking tools, which in this case is the Notepad in the Accessories group within Windows 3.11. If you are using Windows 95, click on *Start*, click *Accessories,* and click *Notepad*. Once you have picked the recipe (structure), collected the ingredients (images) and the cooking tools (Notepad), it is time to cook the dish. We shall begin with the general HTML format.

HTML Tags

The entire HTML program must start with the <html> tag and end with the </html> tag. This informs the browser that the file is written in HTML.

Head and Title Tags

The head and title tags follow the HTML tag. They allow you to describe and identify the page. The title will appear on the blue bar above the *Menu Bar* when viewed in Netscape. For now, limit the title to a few words.

Body Tags

The body tag follows the head and title tags and includes all text and graphics that you would like to show on the page. When combined, it should look like this:

```
<Html>
<Head><title>YOUR TITLE HERE </title> </head>
<body>YOUR TEXT AND GRAPHICS HERE </body>
</html>
```

Formatting the Text and Graphics On Your Page

Insert your text between the <body> and </body> tags. Keep in mind that the browser does not understand the hard carriage return or formatting instructions in Notepad, so you must insert a <br> tag after every line. Otherwise, the computer will read it as one continuous paragraph. If you want a double carriage return, the <p> tag can be utilized. Text can be formatted only in limited ways in HTML. The basic ones are as follows:

Boldface   Boldface a word or a string of words in a sentence by inserting the <b> and </b> tags.

Italics   Italicize a word or a string of words in a sentence by inserting the <i> and </i> tags.

Font Sizes   Control the size of your text by inserting the text between header tags or font size tags. I prefer heading tags as they are easier to control. Allowable font sizes range from H1 to H6, wherein H1 is the largest and H6 is the smallest. To simplify things, we will utilize header tags.

Let's try out the tags by typing the following HTML text into Notepad:

Once upon a time, there was a <b>bold young man </b>who dared to climb the

<i>leaning tower of Pisa.</i> He noticed that as he inched his way up the side of the

tower, the buildings down in the plaza became <h1>smaller</h1> and <h2>smaller</h2>

and <h3>smaller</h3> and <h6>smaller.</h6>

Before going too far in our programming, it would be a good idea to save and view our handiwork. Save your work by taking the following steps:

1. In Notepad, click on *file* on the Menu Bar and choose *save*.
2. Insert your floppy disk in drive A.
3. Beside the word *file name* type **a:home1.htm**

You can then view your work by doing the following:

1. Turn on Netscape by clicking the icon.
2. In Netscape click on *file* on the Menu Bar.
3. Choose *open file.*
4. Beside the word *file name,* type **a:home1.htm**

If something appears wrong, check to make sure that each open <instruction> is matched with a close </instruction>. Develop the habit of saving and viewing your work as you go along.

Carriage or Space Control

As we mentioned earlier, the carriage return in Notepad is not understood by the browser and is therefore ignored. If a string of text is not separated by a divider tag, it will be understood by the browser as continuous. To control line spacing and carriage returns, utilize the following dividers.

Line break or single carriage return. Use the <br> tag to signify the beginning of a line.

Paragraph break or double carriage return. Use the <p> tag to signify the beginning of a new paragraph.

Section break. Use the <hr> tag to create a dividing line between your sections.

Bullets and Numbering

There may be times when you would like to create a bulleted or numbered list. To add a list you must define the beginning and end of the list. Then you would use the <li> tag to create a bullet or number. Here is an example for each. Try them on Notepad, save them and view them in Netscape. Make sure that you do not forget to insert the list within the <body> </body>tags.

Bullets (Unordered List)	Numbering (Ordered List)
The following are my favorite books	Top ten movies this week
<ul>	<ol>
<li> Against the Gods	<li> Conspiracy Theory
<li> A Tale of Two Cities	<li> Godzilla
</ul>	</ol>

The Links
After you have written the text, add links to other documents in your site or to other sites on the Web. The instruction is as follows:

    <a href="URL">anchor text</a>

The URL address or location is invoked when the anchor text is clicked. Hyperlinking documents is the best advantage that the Internet offers, so utilize it. Try typing the sentence below along with the instructions and note that when viewed, the anchor text will appear blue and underlined (between the body tags). Save and view your work as above and then click the anchor text to see how hyperlinking really works.

I think the best business newspaper online is the <a href="http://www.wsj.com"> Wall Street journal Interactive </a>

Adding Image

You can add image or graphic files into your document. Do so with the follow the instruction:

    <img src="image1.jpg">

This will add the images that you gathered earlier from visiting the graphic libraries. Make sure that the graphic files are saved in the same drive and directory as the HTML file.

Finishing Touches

Before you end your site, you should publicize your e-mail address in your site so that your friends can give you feedback on your site. Do this:

```
<a href="mailto:your_email_address@your_school.edu> Mail me you feedback at

your_email_address@your_school.edu </a>
```

Alignment

HTML allows you to control some of the text alignment (left, right or center). The text alignment can either be put together with the header tags or alone as follows:

```
<h1 align=center>John Online</h1>
<h1> <center> John Online</center></h1>
```

How Do They Do That?

I advise you to go to one of your favorite sites (for example, WSJ Interactive Edition) to view its source code. This can be done by first going to the site you are interested in, clicking on *view* on the Netscape Menu Bar, and choosing **view source**. You will see the program behind the site. Look around and try to understand how it was done. Do not allow yourself to be overwhelmed. Some of the programming codes are long and might appear complicated, but as you go through the program, you will notice that it is actually very simple and that the tags are highly repetitive. Pick **Window** in the Menu Bar to toggle or switch between the site and its program. This is probably the best way to learn how HTML really works. It enables you to enjoy the finished product and study the recipe at the same time.

Sample Site

The following is a sample site that will help you get started. Replace the words inside the parentheses with your own text.

```
<html>
<head> <title>(John) Online</title><head>
<body>
<h2 align=center>This is the personal homepage of (John Wiley) </h1>
I am a <i>(sophomore)</i> in <b>(New York university)</b>. <br>
I major in <b>(Finance and marketing)</b> and would like to work on Wall
Street. My favorite reading material online is the <a
href="http://www.wsj.com">Wall Street Journal Online</a>. I also like
the following sites: <p>
<ul>
<li> <a href="http://www.mtv.com">MTV Online</a>
<li><a href="http://www.yahoo.com">Yahoo</a>
</ul>This is my first time at html programming, please <a
href="mailto:(jwiley997@nyu.edu)">E-mail </a> me with your feedback.
<body>
<html>
```

Modify and embellish the site above. You will find that creating your own Web page is fun and exciting. Best of all, it will be entirely of your own creation. Contact your college's computer science department or computer lab to find out how you can put your pages online.

Appendix 5.1
Basic HTML Tags
(complex and less frequently utilized tags may not be listed)

GENERAL	TAGS	Explanation & uses
HTML Programming	<HTML></HTML>	Must start and end all HTML programs.
Title of the site	<TITLE></TITLE>	Must be in the header
Header	<HEAD></HEAD>	Text in the blue area above the menu bar
Body	<BODY></BODY>	The actual text of the site

TEXT FORMATTING

Heading size	<H#></H#>	Range from 1 to 6
Align Text	<P ALIGN=LEFT|CENTER|RIGHT></P>	
Emphasis	<EM></EM	Similar to bold
Strong Emphasis	<STRONG></STRONG>	Similar to bold
Citation	<CITE></CITE>	Similar to italics
Large Font Size	<BIG></BIG>	Old style html text control
Small Font Size	<SMALL></SMALL	Old style html text control
Bold	<B></B>	**BOLD**
Italic	<I></I>	*ITALICS*
Underline	<U></U>	<u>UNDERLINE</u>
Strikeout	<STRIKE></STRIKE>	~~STRIKEOUT~~
Subscript		SUB_{SCRIPT}
Superscript		$Super^{SCRIPT}$
Preformatted	<PRE></PRE>	(display text spacing as-is)
Width	<PRE WIDTH=#></PRE>	
Center	<CENTER></CENTER>	
Blinking	<BLINK></BLINK>	Never use this; I hate this!
Font Size	<FONT SIZE=#></FONT>	Ranges from 1-7
Change Font Size	<FONT SIZE="+# or -#"></FONT>	Ranges from –7 to +7
Base Font Size	<BASEFONT SIZE=#>	Ranges from 1-7; default is 3
Font Color	<FONT COLOR="#"></FONT>	6-number color hexacode
Font face	<FONT FACE="name"></FONT>	e.g., Courier

HYPERLINKS

Link to another site	<A HREF="URL address"></A>	Replace name with address
Name of target	<A NAME="name"></a>	Name must be unique in a document
Link within the document or part of another document	<A HREF="URL address #name"></A> <A HREF="#name"></A>	(if in another document) (if in current document)

IMAGE FORMATTING

Image display	<IMG SRC="URL">	Http:// or File://
Text Alternate	<IMG SRC=" URL" ALT="text">	(text when the image cannot be displayed)
Image Dimensions	<IMG SRC=" URL" WIDTH=# HEIGHT=#>	In number of pixels
Image Border	<IMG SRC=" URL" BORDER=#>	Thickness of border in number of pixels
Horizontal Space b/w image and text	<IMG SRC="URL" HSPACE=#>	In number of pixels
Vertical Space b/w image and text	<IMG SRC="URL" VSPACE=#>	In number of pixels
Imagemap	<IMG SRC="URL" ISMAP>	(allows for clickable maps)

DIVIDERS

Paragraph	<P></P>	A double carriage return
Line Break	 	A single carriage return
Horizontal Rule	<HR>	A dividing line
Alignment	<HR ALIGN=LEFT|RIGHT|CENTER>	
Thickness	<HR SIZE=#>	In number of pixels
Width	<HR WIDTH=#>	In number of pixels
Solid Line	<HR NOSHADE>	

LISTS

Unordered List (bullets)	<UL><LI></UL>	<LI> before each list bullet
Ordered List (numbering)	<OL><LI></OL>	<LI> before each list bullet
Definition List	<DL><DT><DD></DL>	<DT>=term, <DD>=definition
Directory List	<DIR><LI></DIR>	<LI> before each list bullet

BACKGROUNDS AND COLORS

Tiled Background	<BODY BACKGROUND="URL">	
Background Color	<BODY BGCOLOR="#hexacode">	Hexacodes are 6-digit color codes; standard utilized on the web.
Text Color	<BODY TEXT="#hexacode">	
Link Color	<BODY LINK="#hexacode">	
Visited Link	<BODY VLINK="#hexacode">	
Active Link	<BODY ALINK="#$hexacode">	

SPECIAL CHARACTERS

<	&lt;
>	&gt;
&	&amp;
"	&quot;

Registered TM	&reg;
Copyright	&copy;
Non-Breaking Space	

TABLES

Define Table	\<TABLE\>\</TABLE\>
Table Border	\<TABLE BORDER\>\</TABLE\>
Table Border	\<TABLE BORDER=#\>\</TABLE\>
Table Width in Pixels	\<TABLE WIDTH=#\>
Table Width in Percent	\<TABLE WIDTH\>
Table Row	\<TR\>\</TR\>
Row Horizontal Alignment	\<TR ALIGN=LEFT|RIGHT|CENTER\>
Row Vertical Alignment	\<VALIGN=TOP|MIDDLE|BOTTOM\>
Table Cell	\<TD\>\</TD\>
Cell Horizontal Alignment	\<TD ALIGN=LEFT|RIGHT|CENTER\>
Cell Vertical Alignment	\<VALIGN=TOP|MIDDLE|BOTTOM\>
Cell/Columns horizontal size	\<TD COLSPAN=#\>
Cell/Columns vertical size	\<TD ROWSPAN=#\>
Cell/Columns Width in pixels	\<TD WIDTH=#\>
Cell/Columns Width in Percent	\<TD WIDTH="%"\>
Cell/Columns Color	\<TD BGCOLOR="#hexacode"\>

FRAMES

Frame Document	\<FRAMESET\>\</FRAMESET\>	Start and end frame insert
Row Heights	\<FRAMESET ROWS=,,,\>\</FRAMESET\>	
Row Heights	\<FRAMESET ROWS=*\>\</FRAMESET\>	Percentage of viewing size
Borders	\<FRAMESET FRAMEBORDER="yes|no"\>	Either YES or NO
Border Width	\<FRAMESET BORDER=#\>	
Border Color	\<FRAMESET BORDERCOLOR="#hexacode"\>	
Define Frame	\<FRAME\>(contents of an individual frame)	
Display Document	\<FRAME SRC="URL"\>	
Frame Name	\<FRAME NAME="name"|_blank|_self|_parent|_top \>	
Margin Width	\<FRAME MARGINWIDTH=#\>	
Margin Height	\<FRAME MARGINHEIGHT=#\>	
Scrollbar?	\<FRAME SCROLLING="YES|NO|AUTO"\>	
Not Resizable	\<FRAME NORESIZE\>	

MISCELLANEOUS

Java Applet	\<APPLET\>\</APPLET\>
Author's Address	\<ADDRESS\>\</ADDRESS\>

Chapter 6
Business Extra

Business Extra gives you access to current articles from the *Journal* dealing with all aspects of today's business world. The articles on this site are organized by discipline, and are updated every two weeks. While you may be using this service for a particular course, you are encouraged to view articles in the other business disciplines as well.

Registering for Business Extra

In order to access the information on this site, you need to first register, following the steps below:

1. Open your browser, connect to the internet, and go to:

    http://www.wiley.com/college/businessextra

2. From the main screen, click on the "Register" button. Read the **Dow Jones Terms and Conditions**, and if you accept, click on "I Accept" at the bottom of the screen.

3. Type the name of your school in the space provided, and press "Find School"

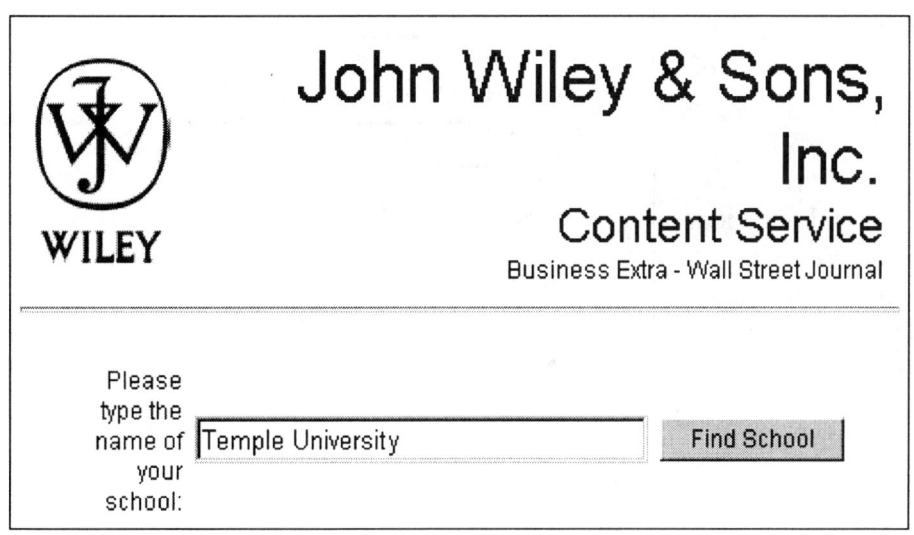

4. In the "Registration Code" field, enter the 17-digit number from the tear-out card in the front of your "On-Line Business Survival Guide", being sure to enter the hyphens as they appear in the numbers.

5. Complete the remainder of the registration process, being sure to fill in all the fields with asterisks. You will create <u>your own</u> Username and Password. Be sure to write these on the spaces provided on the tear-out card, for future reference.

6. When you have compeleted the form, click the "Register" button at the bottom of the screen.

7. You will receive a notice of authorization. Click on "Access Content" to begin using the site.

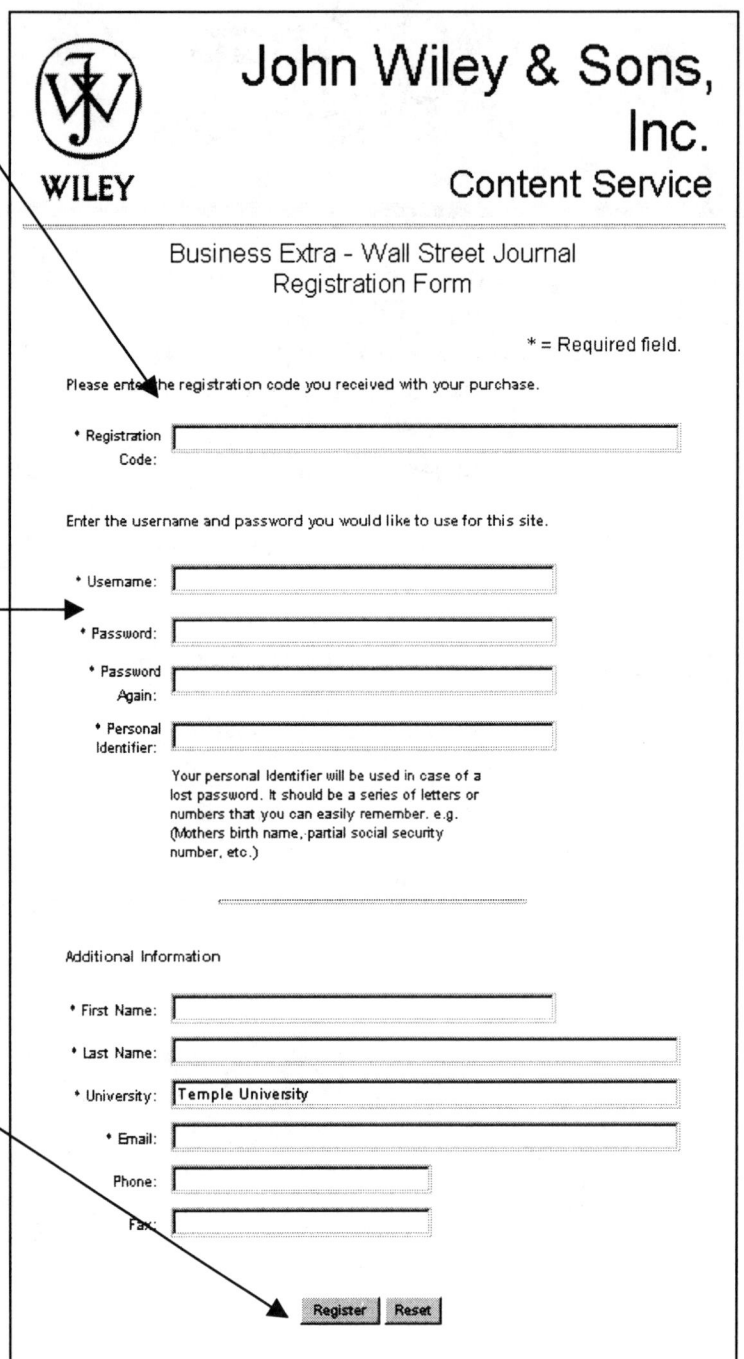

John Wiley & Sons, Inc.
Content Service

Business Extra - Wall Street Journal
Registration Form

* = Required field.

Please enter the registration code you received with your purchase.

* Registration Code:

Enter the username and password you would like to use for this site.

* Username:

* Password:

* Password Again:

* Personal Identifier:

Your personal Identifier will be used in case of a lost password. It should be a series of letters or numbers that you can easily remember. e.g. (Mothers birth name, partial social security number, etc.)

Additional Information

* First Name:

* Last Name:

* University: Temple University

* Email:

Phone:

Fax:

Register   Reset

Using Business Extra

From the main screen, you can select your discipline by clicking on it in the left-hand bar.

! **Note:** If you are using AOL, you may need to download another browser to take full benefit of Business Extra. The site is designed with some advanced features that AOL is unable to handle. If you click on "AOL Users Click Here" on the main screen, you will find step-by-step instructions on how to download another browswer.

The next screen lists the available articles, broken down into two parts. "New For this Update" includes the newest articles posted to the site (updated every two weeks). The "Library" includes the articles from previous updates.

To access an article, simply click on the title. You will be prompted to enter your Username and Password, and then the article will appear in a new window.

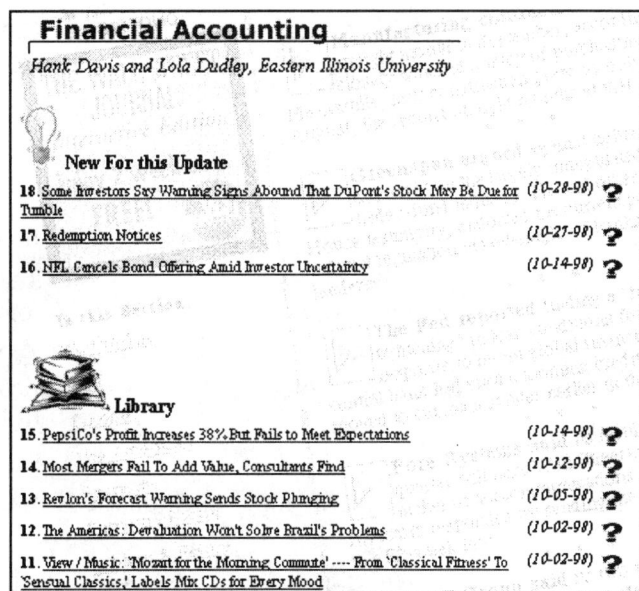

Answering Questions

Each article on Business Extra is accompanied by a series of questions for further exploration. You may use these on your own, or your professor may encourage you to respond to the questions and give your answers to him or her.

To access the questions, click on the question mark next to each article. This question mark appears both on the index page and at the top of each article page.

The questions come up in a box, with space provided for you to type your responses. Once you have entered the responses to your satisfaction, you can either print the page to turn in, or e-mail your answers to your professor by completing the information at the bottom of the page, and clicking "Submit My Answers".

You will receive a notification that your response has been successfully delivered.

! **Note:** It is probably a good idea to print your answers anyway at this point, to make sure you retain a copy of them.

Links

Because there is a wealth of information available on the Web, one challenge can be simply finding the sites that are relevant to your needs and organizing that information. We have included in this chapter a compilation and description of useful Web sites, so that you can quickly and easily begin your search. However, a great place to begin your search is at Wiley's **Business Extra** Web site. All the links included in this chapter are available through this site.

To access the links on the site, simply click on the "Links" button in the navigation bar:

General Sites

American Marketing Association
http://www.ama.org
Listing of resources in marketing including classifieds for jobs and other opportunities, research publications, conferences, membership and more.

American Stock Exchange
http://www.amex.com
This site gives updated news, market summary, and company listings of the American Stock Exchange. There is also an interactive electronic information resource, which offers insights from influential business leaders on major issues tied to the capital markets.

Asia Pacific Management Forum
http://www.mcb.co.uk/ampforum/nethome.htm
A site for networking, resources on Asia Pacific Organizations, Business, and management development

AT&T Business Network
http://www.bnet.att.com
Contains searchable databases and links on virtually all business subjects. Includes thousands of industry and marketing analyses, company web page "Yellow Pages", investor databases including annual reports and regional business resources.

The Business Incorporating Guide
http://www.corporate.com
An online service to help business people, lawyers, and accountants from corporations. Also has links to INC. Online magazine and other small business related sites.

Business Information Service on Newly Independent States
http://www.itaiep.doc.gov/bisnis/nisnis.html
The site provides information on a variety of topics that are of concern with the emerging market countires (ex: Kazakstan). Topics include eocnomic overviews, regulatory issues, foreign investment analysis, trade issues among other pertinent items for global decision makers.

A Business Researcher's Interests - Organizations and Information & Business and Technology
http://www.pitt.edu/~malhotra/interest.html
A site containing information for researchers, academics, and practitioners of Information Processes, Information Systems, and Information Technology relevant to contemporary organizations. Includes full text papers, magazine and journal articles, case studies, and links.

Business Summary
http://www.yahoo.com/headlines/business/
Updates of business headlines.

Capital Quest - Entrepreneurs in Search of Funding
http://www.usbusiness.com/capquest/home.html
This site provides entrepreneurs an alternative to venture capital firms. Potential investors can choose from over twenty industries to invest in including: biotechnology, computer, publishing, retailing, etc.

Capital Venture Home Page
http://www.capitalventure.com/articles
A detailed description of Venture Capital, including several articles on the subject.

CommerceNet Consortium
http://www.commerce.net/
CommerceNet is an industry consortium comprised of over 150 businesses dedicated to the development of Internet commerce. This site provides information on acheiving success in the Internet Market.

Contact Network
http://www.contact.org/dir.htm
A site containing a list of international and domestic nonprofit organizations that can be searched by country, state or issue. Contains links to many nonprofit organizations' sites.

Corporate Financials Online
http://www.cfonews.com/
This company posts financial information from publicly traded companies. Information includes recent news, earnings, dividends and shareholder information.

Currency Converter
http://www.olsen.ch/cgi-bin/exmenu
The Olsen & Associates currency converter allow you to find out the foreign exchange rates from a variety of world currencies.

Excite Business
http://www.excite.com/Reviews/Business/Jobs/index.html
Another starting point to conduct an online job search.

Fannie Mae
http://www.fanniemae.com/
Information about their company and the nation's housing finance system. Mortgage lenders will learn how to do business with Fannie Mae while prospective home buyers will find a whole range of mortgage 'how-to' information.

Fidelity Investments Investor Center
http://www.fid-inv.com
Features useful information and easy-to-use interactive investor tools. Can request information on mutual funds, use investor tools such as worksheets, and find out about upcoming seminars,

and many other topics of interest. Can also download software and enter the "Guess the Dow" contest.

Financial Support Services, Inc.
http://www.turbosales.com/~sfbj/finsupp.html
Helps small and medium sized companies grow by helping them prepare business and financial plans in order to meet and exceed their goals. Includes services such as loan requests, joint venture proposals, financial forecasting, capital planning, and more.

Foreign Exchange Rates
http://www.wsdinc.com/pgswww/w7037.shtml
A site containing exchange rates which are updated hourly.

Foreign Languages for Travelers
http://www.travelang.com/languages/
Contains more than 30 different language options to give user-friendly translation to help traveling. Provides many links to information about traveling and language sites, such as on-line dictionaries.

Frontiers of Entrepreneurship Research
http://www.babson.edu/entrep/re.html#fme
The Frontiers of Entrepreneurship Research is the title of a series of publications which comprise the most comprehensive collection of empirical research papers on entrepreneurship available. These papers are selected from those presented at the annual Babson College-Kauffman Foundation Entrepreneurship Research Conference.

General Motors: People in Motion
http://www.gm.com/index.cgi
Whether you're looking for information regarding GM's financial performance or just want to know what options might be available on that new car you're planning to buy after you graduate, this homepage has it all!

GNN Personal Finance Center
http://www.gnn.com/meta/finance
The GNN Personal Finance Center WWW site provides references and documents on investments and personal income. Users will find guides for money management and investments in new markets.

Heroz Enterprises, Inc. - Champions of Success for Home-based & Small Businesses
http://tucson.com/heroz/
If you're not sure your job will exist in five years or if you dream of being your own boss, this homepage will provide you will plenty of helpful tips and reminders for how to plan, finance, and ultimately initiate your own business.

Hoover's Online
http://www.hoovers.com/
An online version of the Hoover's handbook on companies. This online service provides access to company profiles and company financials as well as job listings and links to over 2800 company web sites.

Interactive Investors
http://www.iii.co.uk/
A site containing a variety of financial information useful for anyone in the financial services industry. Available information ranges includes news, price quotes, advice and more.

Merrill Lynch, Pierce, Fenner & Smith
http://www.ml.com/
Provides extensive coverage of the investment company's services, such as retirement planning, stock investments, mutual funds, and business investments. Sub-directories include: Investor Learning Center, Personal Finance Center, Business Planning Center, and the Financial News & Research Center.

National Corporate Services
http://www.csn.net/natcorp/index.html
A nicely organized and reasonably comprehensive browsing point for financial information on the web. This site contains virtually all financial sources including thousands of companies' financial data.

National Mortgage Loan Directory
http://www.mortgageloan.com/national.html
A site containing quotes for mortgage rates around the country. You can search this index by state and city to compare loan rates of different mortgage companies regionally.

The New York Society of Security Analysts
http://www.nyssa.org/
The New York Society of Security Analysts has provided and has been the premier forum in the United States for the exchange of investment information between senior corporate officials and financial analysts, portfolio managers and others involved in the investment decision making process. The Mission of the New York Society of Security Analysts (NYSSA) is to serve the needs of all professionals involved in the investment decision-making process and to assist and educate the investing public.

NLightN
http://www.nlightn.com/index.htm
Use this free service to locate data stored in more than 500 public and private databases, news services, and the Internet.

Online Services for Industry
http://www.industry.net/
A site that tries to simplify the buying and selling process. This site is based on the fact that the best way to do that is to bring the buyers and the sellers together in a dynamic, interactive environment. This is an online industry that provides links to catalogs, brochures and news items.

PAWWS Financial Network
http://www.pawws.secapl.com/invest.html
The Net Investor is a convenient new way to manage your investments that gives you more control over your brokerage account than ever before. It provides 24-hour, online access to true low-cost trading and the tools you need to effectively manage your portfolio.

The PointCast Network
http://www.pointcast.com
PointCast is an Internet news network that can be used as a screen saver and updated as often as you would like. This site includes world news, as well as information on any industries you choose. Also, there is sports, entertainment ands weather news.

Research Databases (link page)
http://www-leland.stanford.edu/~doncram/crsp.html
This site is basically a link page to research databases along with additional information. Most of the databases are for local users but this is a good place to start when looking for research information. Included are the CRSP as well as Wharton databases.

Resources at Thurderbird (American Graduate School of Management)
http://www.t-bird.edu
A site containing a huge, searchable list of links to other sites with useful information for people who are interested in international business and opportunities.

Resources for Business
http://www.aristotle.net/business/buslink.html
This site provides useful access to variety information categories which are useful for businessperson. The first category is Markets which offer links to various financial markets including updates and analysis. The second is Corporate Web Sites that is linked to many big and successful companies' homepages. Thirdly, Publications, this group provides list of links to valuable business and world information from world class sources and experts.

Resources for International Economics
http://nmg.clever.net/wew/index.html
Macro economic information for all areas of the world. The site includes everything from industrial production, labor markets, commodities, trade information, foreign exchange rates, etc.

Russian Business & Trade Connections
http://www.publications-etc.com/russia/business/
A monthly journal on business trade, and investment in Russia and the CIS. Lists business proposals and company annual reports.

Sallie Mae
http://www.saliemae.com
This site includes information for college students on student loans including a 'loan calculator' to help you calculate your loan payments once you leave school.

Silicon Investor
http://www.techstocks.com/
A site containing huge sources of information on the highly volatile technology industry.

Sports Marketing
http://biz.voregion.edu/sportsmark/sportsmeent.html
This site provides information regarding the different aspects of sports marketing. It also provides links to various sports pages.

Thurderbird (American Graduate School of Management)
http://www.t-bird.edu
A site containing a huge, searchable list of links to other sites with useful information for people who are interested in international business and opportunities.

Vanguard Investor Education Center
http://www.vanguard.com/educ/inveduc.html
Great site! Provides tutorials on mutual funds, stocks, investments and is easy to read and understand. Discusses how to read mutual fund documents, how to build your portfolio and how to evaluate mutual funds. Also includes an Investment Personality Profile to assess your acceptance level of risk.

Wall Street Research Net
http://www.wsrn.com
Useful links to help professional and private investors perform fundamental research on actively traded companies and mutual funds and locate important economic data that moves markets. Among other things there are business news, foreign exchange rates, monetary indicators and reviews of current publications.

Women in Technology International
http://www.witi.com/
Homepage for WITI, which is a professional organization for women working in the high-tech sector. Career opportunities, professional development articles, and more.

Worldwide Banking Guide
http://www.qualisteam.com/aconf.html
Links to nearly 800 bank home pages worldwide, listed by country.

Yahoo: Small Business and Economy: Small Business and Information: Venture Capital
http://my.yahoo.com/Business_and_Economy/Small_Business_Information/Venture_Capital/
This is Yahoo's top level directory for venture capital sites. Among the useful links it has is Price Waterhouse's quarterly survey of the venture capital industry.

Accounting

- National Accounting Associations
- The Big Six

National Accounting Associations

It is very important for professions such as yourself to put your name in the market. The best way to do this is to join associations that interest you the most. Some associations listed below provide free membership and an e-mail listing. If you are not yet sure which accounting field you would like to focus on, we suggest that you check what your profession will look like beforehand. These associations even provide e-mail addresses and names of professionals in your area that you may be able to contact and have discussions with.

Most of these sites provide their members with important support, as follows:

Peer support
Conferences and seminars to increase understanding and knowledge of the subject area
Career guidance and support
Scholarships
Technical support
Newsletters

Academy of Accounting Historian
http://weatherhead.cwru.edu/Accounting/
The objectives of the Academy are to encourage research, publication, teaching, and personal interchanges in all phases of Accounting History and its interrelation with business and economic history.

American Accounting Association
http://www.rutgers.edu/Accounting/raw/aaa/aaa.htm
The Association as defined by the site is "a voluntary organization of persons interested in accounting education and research. Full members receive the Association's newsletter, Accounting Education News, and at least one of the Association's three main journals: The Accounting Review, Accounting Horizons, or Issues in Accounting Education.

American Institute of Certified Public Accountants
http://www.aicpa.org/index.htm
With more than 330,000 members, the AICPA is one of the premier national professional associations for CPAs in the U.S. Like other sites, this site was designed to enhance the effectiveness of the Institute's communications with its members.

Association of Chartered Accountants in the United States
http://ourworld.compuserve.com/homepages/acaus
ACAUS is the not-for-profit professional organization representing the interests of the 5,000 U.S.-based chartered accountants from institutes in Australia, Canada, England and Wales, Ireland, New Zealand, Scotland, and South Africa.

American Society of Women Accountants
http://www.aswa.org

Beta Alpha Psi – The National Accounting Fraternity
http://www.bap.org
Beta Alpha Psi is one of the premier national scholastic and professional accounting fraternities in the U.S. The objective of this group is to encourage and give recognition to scholastic and professional excellence in the field of accounting. This includes promoting the study and practice of accounting; providing opportunities for self-development and association among members and practicing accounting; and encouraging a sense of ethical, social, and public responsibility.

Florida Society of Accounting and Tax Professionals
http://www.web4u.com/fsatp
Its goal is to defend the right to practice, the education of its members, and pride in its professions. The Society accomplishes these goals through the membership requirements and continuing education requirements. The Society has 11 districts and 21 chapters throughout the state to serve its members.

International Association of Hospitality Accountants
http://www.iaha.org
A society for financial and MIS professionals in the hospitality industry, it has more than 3,800 members from around the world.

NALGA – National Association of Local Government Auditors
http://www.libertynet.org/~nalga
NALGA is a professional organization to improve local government auditing.

National Association of State Boards of Accountancy
http://www.nasba.org
This organization tries to provide high-quality, effective programs and services. It identifies, researches, and analyzes major, current and emerging issues affecting state boards of accountancy. It aims to strengthen and maintain communications with member boards and develop and foster relationship with organizations that impact the regulation of public accounting.

The "Big Six" Accounting Firms

Arthur Andersen
http://www.arthurandersen.com/

Coopers & Lybrand L.L.P.
http://www.colybrand.com/

Deloite & Touche
http://www.dttus.com/home.htm

Ernst & Young L.L.P.
http://www.ey.com/us/

KPMG Peat Marwick
http://www.us.kpmg.com/

Price Waterhouse
http://www.pw.com/us/

Decision Sciences

Operations Management Index
http://www.wbs.warwick.ac.uk/omindex

OM-Info Master Matrix
http://www.muohio.edu/~bjfinch/ommatrix.html

INFORMS
http://www.informs.org

Decision Sciences Institute (DSI)
http://www.dsi.gsu.edu

Production and Operations Management Society (POMS)
http://www.poms.org

American Society for Quality (ASQ)
http://www.asq.org

Educational Society for Resource Management (APICS)
http://www.apics.org

Cornell University, Peter Jackson
http://www.orie.cornell.edu/~jackson

Drake University, Brad Meyer
http://www.cbpa.drake.edu/meyer

Manufacturing Systems
http://www.manufacturingsystems.com
This is the site for Manufacturing Systems Magazine. It focuses on manufacturing information systems, including new technology developments and case studies. The site also contains selected articles not included in the magazine as well as links to other related sites.

Finance Links

American Stock Exchange
http://www.amex.com
This site gives updated news, market summary, and company listings of the American Stock Exchange. There is also an interactive electronic information resource, which offers insights from influential business leaders on major issues tied to the capital markets.

The Association for Investment Management and Research
http://www.aimr.com/aimr.html
The Association for Investment Management and Research is an international, nonprofit organization of investment. AIMR, through the ICFA, grants the prestigious Chartered Financial Analyst (CFA®) designation. In addition, AIMR is dedicated to sustaining high standards of ethical and professional conduct among its members and seeks to extend these standards throughout the investment community practitioners and educators.

Bank Rate Monitoring
http://www.bankrate.com/
Current bank rate information on mortgages, CDs, money market funds, and other

CNNFN Stock Quotes
http://www.cnnfn.com/markets/quotes.html
Provides stock quotes (high, low, volume, P/E ratio, bid, ask, EPS, 52-week high/low) for specific stock entered into CNNFN's search engine.

Commercial Real Estate Network
http://www.ccim.com/
A site dedicated to facilitating networking and information sharing between our members and the public. The site is sponsored by CIREI, the Commercial Investment Real Estate Institute, an affiliate member of the National Association of Realtors.

Corporate Financials Online
http://www.cfonews.com/
This company posts financial information from publicly traded companies. Information includes recent news, earnings, dividends and shareholder information.

Country Risk Analysis

http://www.duke.edu/~charvey/Country_risk/couindex.htm

A site containing papers and data relating to Risk factors in different countries. It is divided into five sections:

1.) Exploratory Investigation of Country Returns
2.) Expected Returns and Volatility in 135 Markets: Background
3.) Political Risk, Economic Risk and Financial Risk
4.) The Behavior of Emerging Market Returns
5.) The Challenges of Emerging Markets Data

Deutsche Bank Homepage

http://www.deutsche-bank.de/db/gb95e/ib4.html

This site provides information about Deutsche Bank, its performance and its future outlook.

Emerging Markets Companion

http://www.emgmkts.com/toc/toc.html

Investment and financial information on emerging markets worldwide. Available information ranges from security prices and research reports to political, economic and financial news that affect markets and businesses.

The Euroclear IFR Handbook of World Stock and Commodity Exchanges 1995

http://www.lpac.ac.uk/ifr/

Information on 250 exchanges worldwide, including address/fax/phone, names of key contacts, history, hours/holidays, organizational structure, market capitalization, turnover, taxes and regulatory structure. The site is designed to meet the needs of traders, brokers, bankers, treasurers, analysts and fund managers, among others.

Financial Markets

http://gopher.great-lakes.net:2200/1/partners/ChicagoFed/finance

Monthly and daily time series rates on T-bills, notes, commercial papers, certificates of deposit, exchange rates, and money supply.

FINWEB - A financial economics WWW server

http://risknet.com/finweb.html

List of Internet resources providing substantive information concerning economics and finance related topics.

Foreign Exchange Rates

http://www.wsdinc.com/pgswww/w7037.shtml

A site containing exchange rates which are updated hourly.

Fred -- Federal Reserve Economic Data

http://www.stls.frb.org/fred/

This site is the St. Louis Federal Reserve Bank's version of the Fred database of historic economic information. Also included is access to a variety of current economic research.

Fundlink
http://www.wcbcom.com/~fundlink/
A comprehensive list of mutual funds as well as various performance statistics and a guide to investing.

HomeOwners Finance Center
http://www.homeowners.com/homeowners/in-magellan.html
A site containing the latest interest rates, market trends, adjustable rate indices, a mortgage calculator, discussions about loan strategies, and online forms for purchasing and refinancing.

Interactive Investors
http://www.iii.co.uk/
Available information ranges includes news, price quotes, advice and more.

International Monetary Fund
gopher://gopher.imf.org
This site contains information on the IMF, country reports, information on finance and development, and other related organizations.

International Trade Law Monitor
http://itl.irv.uit.no/trade-law/
A searchable list of subjects concerning international trade law with links to detailed and useful information for people who may e involved in international trade or global business.

Internet Economic and Statistics Resources
http://www.lib.isu.edu/bus/economic.html
Economic and statistical information gathered by the Federal Reserve Board, as well as tables of contents form scholarly publications.

The Internet Resource Center for Derivatives
http://www.numa.com/derivs/drivex.html
This web site is dedicated to providing information and resources for those interested in derivatives. The contents include option strategies, derivatives FAQ, WWW directory of futures & options exchanges, etc.

I.Q. Chart
http://www.iqc.com
Incredible resource for technical analysis of stocks. Includes both basic and very advanced techniques. Most useful function is that it will search for all stocks that fit your technical parameters. Also has option pricing model.

Investment FAQ
http://www.cis.ohio-state.edu/hypertext/faq/usenet/investment-faq/general/top.html
This list of frequently asked questions and answers is an excellent introduction to investing.

Invest-o-rama
http://www.investorama.com
A leading Internet directory for investors. Investment information consisting of investing links, featured articles, stocks to watch, and educational center.

The IPO Network
http://www.ipo-network.com/
Contains information on IPOs and upcoming IPOs. Provides prospectus summaries, an IPO calendar, and information on underwriting firms. Also allows the user to get stock quotes.

Japan Search Engine
http://www1.nisiq.net/~jsengine/eng/economy/markets/index.html
Contains links to Japanese investment & market information, industry, Japanese bond market information and Japanese stock market information.

J. P. Morgan
http://www.jpmorgan.com/
Coverage of emerging markets, commodities, government bonds, asset management, and more. J.P. Morgan is a global financial services firm that serves governments, corporations, institutions, individuals and privately held firms.

La Bourse de Paris
http://www.bourse-de-Paris.fr/
A site which contains information and statistics about the main financial players in the French Market and exchange information.

Market Guide
http://www.marketguide.com/
The Market Guide Investment Center is a comprehensive business web site designed to provide a wealth of investment and financial information, including research reports on over 8,300 publicly traded companies.

Merrill Lynch, Pierce, Fenner & Smith
http://www.ml.com/
Provides extensive coverage of the investment company's services, such as retirement planning, stock investments, mutual funds, and business investments. Sub-directories include: Investor Learning Center, Personal Finance Center, Business Planning Center, and the Financial News & Research Center.

Money Quick Quotes
http://quote.pathfinder.com/money/quote/qc
An index of stock quotes and reports. Provide listings for the Dow Jones Industrial Average Index, the S&P 500 Index, and the S&P Mindcap Index.

NETworth
http://networth.galt.com
A site containing both stock and mutual fund information. Each user is allowed to create a personal portfolio for no cost. This information is updated every 15 minutes during trading hours. It tracks most recent trading price, days gain/loss, total % gain/loss for holding period and total value of portfolio. Graphs can also be created for various time frames for individual stocks. Stocks can be traded on the NYSE, AMEX, NASDAQ, TORONTO, MONTREAL, ALBERTA, and CANADIAN OVER-THE-COUNTER.

The New York Society of Security Analysts
http://www.nyssa.org/
The New York Society of Security Analysts has provided and has been the premier forum in the United States for the exchange of investment information between senior corporate officials and financial analysts, portfolio managers and others involved in the investment decision making process.

Nikkei Net
http://www.nikkei.co.jp
This Japanese site, which also has an English translation, is packed with information such as stock market data, economic news, and corporate updates. It allows users to keep up with business activities in Japan daily through English translations of stories from the Nihon Keizai Shimban, a Japanese newspaper.

PAWWS Financial Network
http://www.pawws.secapl.com/invest.html
It provides 24-hour, online access to true low-cost trading and the tools you need to effectively manage your portfolio.

Quote
http://www.fastquote.com/fq/quotecom/quote
Contains a lot of information about the most recent prices of stock. It also shows relevant financial information through multiple charts.

The Real Estate Cyberdistrict
http://home.earthlink.net/~wedge/
This site is devoted to commercial real estate. Information topics include lenders, REITs, developers, properties, and perhaps most importantly, job listings.

Reuters Finance Link Page
http://www.synrsoft.com/pages/finance.html
Site provides information about commodities, derivatives and financial futures. Contains recent updates of the various commodities markets.

Russian Exchange

http://www.fe.nsk.ru/infomarket/

A site containing and explaining the creation of the Russian Commodity and Raw Materials Exchange. Contains lists of links to news at the Russian Exchange, weekly review of markets, daily auction results and much more.

Schwab Investments Homepage

http://www.scwhab.com

Allows on-line trading with low commission. Also, provides investment experts' advice about international investing. You can also do on-line research from the site.

Security APL

http://www.secapl.com/cgi-bin/qs/

Security APL offers portfolio management systems and service to the investment advisory, brokerage and banking industries. Security APL designs custom solutions with clients, allowing investment managers the kind of functionality that increases productivity.

Smith Barney Stock Exchange

http://nestegg.iddis.com/smithbarney/stock.html

A site which provides timely investment advise and market analysis. Available information ranges from current research headlines to historical data of stocks covered by Smith Barney.

Sources of Finance for Trade and Investment in the NIS

http://www.itaiep.doc.gov/bisnis/finance/finance.html

This site contains information about U.S. Government Agencies which assist U. S. companies in finding financing in the newly independent states of the former USSR. It has links to governmental, private and educational places to locate financing.

Stock Rates at the Major Asian Markets

http://itlnet.com/moneypages/syndicate/nfunds/funds.html

Current stock rates from all the major Asian stock markets are listed and updated at the top of the hour.

Stockmaster

http://www.stockmaster.com

A site containing stock information that serves individual investors with stock and mutual fun quotes and historical charts since 1993.

Trendwatch Subscribers Page

http://www.trendwatch.com/

Trendwatch keeps an eye on individual stocks traded on NYSE, ASE, and NASDAQ. Any potential broker or investor can look here for a second opinion.

Vanguard Investor Education Center

http://www.vanguard.com/educ/inveduc.html

Provides tutorials on mutual funds, stocks, investments and is easy to read and understand. Discusses how to read mutual fund documents, how to build your portfolio and how to evaluate mutual funds. Also includes an Investment Personality Profile to assess your acceptance level of risk.

Wall Street Research Net

http://www.wsrn.com

Perform fundamental research on actively traded companies and mutual funds and locate important economic data that moves markets. Among other things there are business news, foreign exchange rates, monetary indicators and reviews of current publications.

World Economic Window

http://www.nmg.clerver.net./wew/index.html

This site provides information about economic growth, inflation, exchange rates, balance of payments, etc. for EC and other countries.

Information Systems

- General Information Systems Sites
- Industry Publications
- Standardization of Web Technology
- Languages
- Major Software Makers

General Information Systems Sites

CNET Central

http://www.cnet.com

This is one of the most complete sites for Web technology information that you can find on the Web. The site has not only great reviews for both software and hardware, it also has a download site to get the program discussed. CNET also has other services such as follows:

News.com – on-the-edge Web technology news and press releases
Builder.com - reviews and information for budding and professional Web developers
Gamecenter.com - Download.com and Shareware.com provide the user with one of the most complete and up-to-date sites for downloading software and demos
Axtivex.com - Microsoft Explorer's developers' and users' favorite site

Digital Marketplace

http://www.dgtlmrktplce.com

This site provides information about companies and projects in areas related to: entrepreneurship, communications, manufacturing and engineering, and healthcare and biotech. The part of this site that is of most use to me, however, is the section that provides information about private equity firms. The site divides these firms into everything from buyout funds to commercial banks to merchant bankers to venture capital funds. It is a very useful tool for anyone who is in search of a full-time position in the private equity field.

Hyper Text Markup Language (HTML) v3.2 Reference

http://www2.wvitcoe.wvnet.edu/~sbolt/html3/

Complete reference on HTML including past versions and popular extensions. Good source for those interested in building their own web page.

ISWorld Net Home Page

http://www.isworld.org/isworld/isworldtext.html

Site containing many links to other sites relating to the "creation and dissemination of information systems knowledge". Includes a "What's New" section, discussion groups, links to associations, and sponsors.

Java Computing in the Enterprise

http://www.sun.com/javacomputing

White paper on-line that explains how Java can change computing enterprises.

Jumbo!

http://www.jumbo.com/

A site that offers over 72,906 shareware and freeware programs. Software spans from spreadsheets, wordprocessors, business applications, to games!

Plug-IN Datamation

http://www.datamation.com/

This site has become one of my favorite general sites. I was informed of this site by my colleague L. Ji, who is a technology expert herself. She believes the Datamation site should be the first general site mentioned due to its completeness. The IS workbench provided in this site has the following important IS topics and is supported by the giants in each respective industry:

Year 2000 problem - by Viasoft
Storage systems - by IBM
Datamart - by Digital
Middleware - by Software AG
Mainframes - by IBM
Data Warehousing - by Microsoft
Datamining & OLAP

ZD NET

http://www.zdnet.com/

A great general site for all computer information. This site includes reviews for both hardware and software products. A great site if you are interested in the all popular technology available in the Web.

Industry Publications

There are so many information and computer related magazine on the web that I shall leave you with only the ones I like. Yahoo as mentioned earlier has probably one of the most complete directory or index of these magazines. The address is as follows:

Index of Magazines for Web surfers:
http://www.yahoo.com/Computers_and_Internet/Magazines/Internet/

LAN Times Online
http://www.lantimes.com/
One of the preeminent networking magazines on the Web. This magazine has a wealth of networking information for both new and professional users. It is a great stop to browse on new technological improvements. This site provides the Microsoft Solution center, Novell training and certification center, and specific articles on IS careers.

Data Management Review
http://dmreview.com/
Important and clear data warehousing information and reviews for Web surfers. This should be the first stop for people who want to buy, use, or upgrade their data-warehousing capabilities. In addition it has links to other sites directly under the topic of data management.

Datawarehouse.com
http://www.data-warehouse.com/
Data-warehouse.com is also an excellent one-stop resource for industry professionals. This site allows users to keep abreast of the latest developments in information systems and data-warehousing technology.

Journal of Management Information Systems
http://rmm-java.stern.nyu.edu/jmis/
This sites purpose is to act as a forum for the presentation of research that advances the practice and understanding of organizational information systems. The journal allows professionals to investigate new modes of information delivery and the changing landscape of information policy-making.

Standardization of Web Technology

DISC
http://www.bsi.org.uk/disc/
DISC is section of the British Standards Institution responsible for standardization in Information and Communications Technologies - ICT . DISC is responsive to your business needs and can help you succeed through standards related information, products, best practice guidelines and services. "As the UK's voice in international and European standardization in ICT we aim to represent fully the broad spectrum of standards users. Come and work with us to make ICT work effectively in your organization and throughout UK industry."

DISA
http://www.disa.org/
DISA is a not-for-profit organization that supports the development and use of EDI standards in electronic commerce. The primary services that this organization provides are operational support for the X12 and UN/EDIFACT standards; maintaining and publishing of EDI standards; and providing educational services. DISA has governmental agencies, Fortune 500 members, and other organizations.

ANSI - American National Standards Institute
http://www.ansi.org/
The American National Standards Institute (ANSI) has been the administrator and coordinator of the U.S. private sector voluntary standardization system for the last 78 years. This site is a must for students interested in the electronic commerce industry. ANSI Online provides the user with convenient access to timely and relevant information on the ANSI Federation and latest national and international standards-related activities.

Association for Information &Image Management International
http://www.aiim.org/
The AIIM has 9000 individual and 600 corporate members. This association has served the document-management industry effectively for the last 50 years. The site will allow you to stay up to date with document-management technologies and standards.

National Committee for Information Technology Standards
http://www.ncits.org/
The mission of NCITS is to produce market-driven voluntary standards in the area of information technology.

NCITS creates standards for the following areas:

- voluntary consensus standards in the areas of multimedia (MPEG/JPEG),
- intercommunication among computing devices and information systems (including the Information Infrastructure, SCSI-2
- interfaces, Geographic Information Systems),
- storage media (hard drives, removable cartridges),
- database (including SQL3),
- security,
- programming languages (such as C++)

Information Research Technology Center
http://itrc.on.ca/
ITRC is a not-for-profit organization that performs allocation of research dollars within the university research community. The center encourages collaboration between the university research community and private industry. The site has the "ask the expert" section that allows students and users to pose questions directly to industry leaders.

Languages

Gamelan
http://www.gamelan.com/
This is the first and last source of Java information on the Web. I believe that Gamelan.com is the most complete directory of resources relating to the Java programming language. The site provides links to Java resources and context. The site also has articles regarding the capacity and current events regarding the Java language. This site has hundreds of links to every conceivable site that has anything to do with Java, Active X, VRML channel, and other emerging technologies. The site is a definite place to visit for anyone interested in Java.

Java World
http://www.javaworld.com/
This is the premiere and official magazine for the Java technology and programming language. I personally think that this site is an excellent way to keep users in touch with the newest uses of the programming language.

Linux Java Tips and Hints Page
http://www.parnasse.com/java.shtml
This site is an informal list of Perl, Java and Linux problem solvers and troubleshooting site. It may have the answer to the nagging bug you have been having, especially for beta versions of programs such as Netscape.

Java & HotJava Info on the Web
http://www.iat.unc.edu/guides/irg-42.html
The site has a list of the following research information

- Articles/Papers
- Bibliographies
- Book
- On-line Books
- Tools
- On-line Seminars
- Magazines/Newsletters
- Conferences

The Java Boutique
http://javaboutique.internet.com/
This site is a great resource for users and developers who would like to add Java Applets to their own Web sites.

Unix World
http://www.unixworld.com/unixworld/
This is a Web-only magazine that provides articles and columns for users, programmers, and system administrators of UNIX operating system.

Unix Review
http://www.unixreview.com/
This site provides help for UNIX professionals and users to develop and administer superior systems and solutions. The Review offers an excellent analysis of the latest UNIX technologies, software developments, products, standards, and UNIX-related business worldwide.

Sun Server
http://www.pcinews.com/business/pci//sun/
The Sun Server site features information for users and prospective users of Sun technology running commercial networking, Internet, and intranet applications. The site also provides case studies on how Sun hardware and software technology can be utilized to drive enterprise-wide, client-server networks.

The Major Software Makers

Microsoft
http://www.microsoft.com
When all have failed, might as well try the producer of the product itself. Microsoft's site has probably the best library of products, and scripts on active X. Look up special active X creators such as liquid motion or liquid reality. Microsoft's site is he best place to find patches and the newest beta versions.

Sun Microsystem
http://www.sun.com/
Just like Microsoft, the Sun site has probably the best and most current articles regarding the Java technology. Just like the Microsoft site, Sun's site is the best place to find patches and the newest Java updates.

Management

- Major Consulting Firms
- Human Resources Management
- Industry Publications

Major Consulting Firms

AT Kearney
http://www.atkearney.com/
The site definition of the company is as follows "Our management consultants work with all facets and levels of an organization, bringing insight and experience that achieve the necessary results to effect real change to a client's competitive position."

Anderson Consulting

http://www.ac.com/

The site has information on careers and national and international seminars. The site defines the firm as follows "Andersen Consulting is a global leader in management and technology consulting. We are known by our clients for our leadership, our determination, our professionalism and our commitment to quality."

Arthur D. Little

http://www.arthurdlittle.com/default.htm

Management consulting at this firm is defined: "Arthur D. Little is built on a century of helping outstanding organizations accelerate their learning and create real value through positive change. Our people's shared knowledge of best practices is built on our extensive experience guiding change in major industries and government agencies around the globe, ensuring that our clients achieve solid, pragmatic results."

Bain & Co.

http://www.rec.bain.com/

The firm is one of the world's leading international strategy consulting firms.

Booz Allen & Hamilton

http://www.bah.com/

A very well designed site with a mother load of management consulting information. The site has reports on specific areas that might be of importance for your research.

Boston Consulting Group

http://www.bcg.com/

One of the best strategy consulting firms in the nation. The site has some information on recruiting and careers.

Deloitte & Touche Consulting group

http://www.dtcg.com/

This is probably the most fun and colorful management consulting site on the web. The site has a wealth of management consulting information that might be of importance to your research.

Gemini Consulting

http://www.gemcon.com/Pages/homefram.html

This site has primarily career information, with some research information.

IBM Consulting Group - Global Services

http://www.ibm.com/services/

This site has career information for globally-minded consultants.

McKinsey & Company

http://www.mckinsey.com/

This company advises top management of some the largest firms in the world about strategy, organization and operation. The publication area has downloadable PDF formatted reports.

Towers Perrin

http://www.towers.com/

One of the best human resource and general management consulting firm in the world. Like the McKinsey site, this site has a lot of information available in their publications area. They also have links and downloadable PDF reports available.

Human Resources Management

AFL-CIO

http://www.aflcio.org/

Major labor federation site. Many US labor unions are members of the AFL-CIO.

American Compensation Association

http://www/ahrm.org/aca/aca.htm

This organization is composed of academics, consultants, and professionals active in design, implementation and management of employee compensation programs.

Americans with Disabilities Act Documents Center

http://janweb.icdi.wvu.edu/kinder/

Links to ADA resources. Includes sites regarding specific disabilities such as HIV/AIDS, cancer, hearing, visual and mobility impairment, as well as alcohol and drug related issues.

Benefits Link

http://www.magicnet.net/benefits/index.html

Information on various employee benefits plans.

Career Mosaic

http://www.careermosaic.com/

Variety of career and job information as well as data on current job opportunities.

Cornell University School of Industrial and Labor Relations

http://www.ilr.cornell.edu/

Extensive collection of resources on labor and human resources, including government reports, databases, as well as Cornell publications and journals.

HR Magazine

http://www.shrm.org/docs/Hrmagazine.html

Monthly publication of the Society for Human Resource Management. Selected articles of interest to HR students.

The Monster Board

http://www.monster.com/

Information resources for HR professionals.

National Business Employment Weekly
http://www.nbew.com/
Job search and career guidance information.

National Labor Relations Borad (NLRB)
http://wwww.doc.gov:80/nlrb/homepg.html
Continuous updates of NLRB decisions

Occupational Safety and Health Administration (OSHA)
http://www.osha.gov/
Home page of the major monitor of the safety and health of US workers and workplace.

Society for Human Resource Management
http://www.shrm.org/
Daily updates and summaries of major developments in the field of human resources.

Industry Publications

Industry Week
http://www.industryweek.com/
On-line magazine for manufacturing management.

Sloan Management Review
http://web.mit.edu/smr-online/
Journal for the management industry. This site is a great way for management students to find new and innovative issues in the management industry.

Strategy & Business
http://www.strategy-business.com/
This is a senior-level business management on-line magazine for intellectual capital. This site presents business strategy insights from top journalists, CEOs, and management consultants. This site is sponsored by Booz Allen and Hamilton.

Success Magazine
http://www.successmagazine.com/
On-line version of Success Magazine, containing articles on management.

Marketing Links

- Marketing Sites
- Industry Publications

Marketing Sites

American Marketing Association
http://www.ama.org
Listing of resources in marketing including classifieds for jobs and other opportunities, research publications, conferences, membership and more.

International Monetary Fund
gopher://gopher.imf.org
This site contains information on the IMF, country reports, information on finance and development, and other related organizations.

International Trade Law Monitor
http://itl.irv.uit.no/trade-law/
Contains a searchable list of subjects concerning international trade law with links to detailed and useful information for international trade or global business.

La Bourse de Paris
http://www.bourse-de-Paris.fr/
Information and statistics about the main financial players in the French Market and exchange information.

Sports Marketing
http://biz.voregion.edu/sportsmark/sportsmeent.html
This site provides information regarding the different aspects of sports marketing. It also provides links to various sports pages.

Tilburg University's Marketing Link
http://cwis.kub.nl/~few/few/be/marketin/journal1.htm
There are more than 50 marketing journals in the Internet. The Tilburg site promises to deliver all or most of the marketing journals both local and international.

University of Texas's Advertising World
http://advweb.cocomm.utexas.edu/world/
One of the most complete and updated link sites for marketing and advertising enthusiasts.

World Economic Window
http://www.nmg.clerver.net./wew/index.html
This site provides information about economic growth, inflation, exchange rates, balance of payments, etc. for EC and other countries.

Industry Publications

Advertising Age
http://www.adage.com/
One of the most widely read marketing magazine in the nation.

Adweek, Brandweek & Mediaweek
http://www.adweek.com/
This site covers the three weekly magazines: Adweek, Brandweek & Mediaweek.

American Demographics Magazine- Consumer trends for business leaders
http://www.demographics.com/Publications/AD/index.htm
AD has marketing articles written by experts in the industry regarding trends in the industry.

Marketing Tools Magazine
http://www.demographics.com/Publications/MT/index.htm
MT's site is part of the American Demographics Internet site.

Forecast
http://www.demographics.com/Publications/FC/index.htm
Forecast's site has not only articles, but also data and graph in HTML format, allowing you to copy the data straight into your spreadsheet or word processor.

Government Agencies and Information Sources

Bureau of Labor Statistics Homepage
http://stats.bls.gov
Contains most commonly requested time series data about employment, unemployment, wages and salaries price indexes, productivity from various surveys, programs, BLS Regional offices, and BLS overall. The data can be sorted by geographical region, by time, and by values.

Securities and Exchange Commission
http://www.sec.gov
The SEC is defined as an independent, nonpartisan quasijudicial regulatory agency with responsibility for administering federal securities laws. The purpose of these laws is to protect investors in securities markets and to ensure that investors have access to disclosure of all material information concerning publicly traded securities. The Commission also regulates firms engaged in the purchase or sale of securities, people who provide investment advice, and investment companies.

Search SEC Edgar Archives
http://www.sec.gov/cgi-bin/srch-edgar
This site allows you to search for SEC filings made by U.S. companies. Filings from 1994-present are available. New filings seem to be uploaded in a timely manner.

Edgar Database of Corporate Information
http://www.sec.gov/edgarhp.htm
Run by the Securities and Exchange Commission, this site contains the most complete financial information on the Web. Data on all listed companies in the United States are available here. However, before utilizing this site, you need to know the difference between a 10K and 8Q. I addition, you must be careful when printing any data you gather, because some 10K filings fill up more than 300 pages.

Governmental Accounting Standards Board
http://www.rutgers.edu/Accounting/raw/gasb
The mission of the Governmental Accounting Standards Board is to "establish and improve standards of state and local governmental accounting and financial reporting that will result in useful information for users of financial reports and guide and educate the public, including issuers, auditors, and users of financial reports."

Department of Energy
http://www.doe.gov
Data on all aspects of energy consumption and production in the United States.

U.S. Department of Labor
http://www.dol.gov/
Links to several department agencies under the Department of Labor supervision.

The Financial Accounting Standards Board
http://www.rutgers.edu/Accounting/raw/fasb
The mission of the Financial Accounting Standards Board is to establish and improve standards of financial accounting and reporting for the guidance and education of the public, including issuers, auditors, and users of financial information."

Federal Reserve Board
http://www.bog.frb.fed.us/
This site provides information about the Federal Reserve, its functions, and members. It provides links to Federal reports and statistical data.

The General Accounting Office
http://www.gao.gov/
The GAO is the investigative arm of Congress in charge of examining matters related to the receipt and disbursement of public funds, and also performs audits and evaluations of government programs and activities.

Internal Revenue Service
http://www.irs.ustreas.gov/
Site for information from the Internal Revenue Service.

The International Trade Administration
http://www.ita.doc.gov/
A site devoted to trade and export issues. Provides national, regional, state, and local trade and export reports and figures. Offers a monthly trade balance analysis as well as updates and details of region-specific trade/export programs and initiatives.

Small Business Administration
http://www.sbaonline.sba.gov/
Articles and resource listings (state and national) concerning small business development.

Thomas Legislative Information on the Internet
http://thomas.loc.gov
An online library of all current government documents courtesy of the Library of Congress.

U.S. Census Bureau
http://www.census.gov/
A good source for social, demographic, and economic information.

U.S. Department of Commerce Homepage
http://www.doc.gov/CommerceHomePage.html
For industry analysis type research this site may prove to be a good source.

United States Treasury
http://www.ustreas.gov/
The mission of the Department of the Treasury is to formulate and recommend economic, fiscal and tax policies; serve as financial agent of the United States Government; enforce the law; protect the President and other officials; and manufacture coins and currency.

The White House Virtual Library
http://whitehouse.gov/WH/welcome.html
A site containing White House press releases, radio addresses, publicly-released documents, Executive orders and other useful information about government practice and policy. Additionally, contains historic national documents such as The General Agreement on Tariffs and Trade and The North American Free Trade Agreement.

Business Publications

Applied Derivatives Trading
http://www.adtrading.com/
Applied Derivatives Trading is a monthly magazine devoted to all aspects of derivatives trading throughout the world. Its aim is to provide information about trading for traders. ADT is published exclusively via the World Wide Web.

Asia, Inc. Online
http://www.asia-inc.com/
Asia, Inc. Online is an electronic version of Asia, Inc., a leading Asia monthly business journal. The web site contains: (1) current financial news; (2) current and past issues of the journal; (3) a collection of articles published by other magazines; and (4) Asia Internet

Barron's On-line
http://www.vestnet.com/
On-line version of the national financial newspaper.

BBC Homepage
http://www.bbcnc.org.uk/
BBC program listings and discussion categorized by interest.

The Daily Yomiuri--On Line
http://www.yomiuri.co.jp/index-e.htm
Top stories of daily news in English from the many Japanese newspapers.

The Economist
http://www.economist.com
The home page of The Economist magazine. Provides excellent coverage of global economic, business, and political issues. Contains selected articles from current issue as well as monthly reviews of related books and multimedia. Offers free e-mail subscriptions to Business This Week and Politics This Week summaries.

Forbes
http://www.forbes.com
Most current issue of Forbes. In addition, it contains a mutual fund report card, which allows you to type in the first few letters of a particular fund. Information on that fund is then provided, including returns over specific time periods.

Fortune Magazine
http://pathfinder.com/@@@VvDwQAoCUTOGbE/fortune/index.html
This site allows people to read the most current issue of Fortune on-line. It also allows for research ranging from growth companies to the Fortune 500.

Futures Online
http://www.futuresmag.com/
An on-line magazine for those who are interested in futures, including information, education for traders forums, daily market updates, and links to many futures-related sites.

Inc. Online
http://www.inc.com/
Web site provided by Inc. magazine for entrepreneurs starting and running their own businesses. Provides information from the magazine and includes access to databases, software, reference materials, consulting services and other new business oriented links.

Kennedy Publications
http://www.kennedyinfo.com/
A site containing reference information for executive job seekers, executive recruiters, management consultants and outplacement and Human Resources professionals. Includes a great on line job search function.

London Times Homepage
http://www.sunday-times.co.uk
Coverage of international news events from the London Times, including detailed reporting from the European markets.

Mutual Funds Magazine On-line
http://www.mfmag.com
This financial publication is printed by the Institute of Econometric Research, a firm founded to apply the discipline of econometrics to the science of financial forecasting. Available information includes investing strategies and market reviews.

The Nihon Keizai Shimbun--Economy & Finance
http://www.nikkei.co.jp/enews/TNKS/Economy_Finance.html
Daily news about Japanese economics and finance in English, from the Japanese newspaper. This site links with the pages such as "Weekly Summary" and "Business Browser."

The Philadelphia Daily News Online
http://www.phillynews.com/pdn/business
The Philadelphia Daily News Online, business section.

The Red Herring
http://www.herring.com/mag/
Archived issues of The Red Herring magazine on-line. The Red Herring magazine is devoted to discussing technology and finance.

Streetnet
http://www.streetnet.com/
Streetnet is the online version of BuySide Magazine, which caters to money managers. It contains in-depth feature articles on different industries, free stock quotes and market updates.

The Washington Post
http://www.washingtonpost.com/
A site contains daily updates from the Washington Post. Many sections including latest news from every states in the U.S. are provided in order to meet various reader' interests. It especially provides congressional insights and updates from Washington D.C.

Employment

Career Mosaic
http://www.careermosaic.com/
Variety of career and job information as well as data on current job opportunities.

Jobpage
http://asa.ugl.lib.unrich.edu/chdocs/employment
This site pulls together the Net's best sources of job openings and career development information, along with a description and evaluation of each resource. This page also allows to submit your resume electronically.

Jobtrack
http://www.jobtrack.com/
Internet job search site. It provides information on job listings, employers, tips on interviewing and resumes, and links to other helpful sites.

Jobs In Consulting
http://www.cob.ohio-state/~fin/jobs/consult.htm
Information for individuals interested in a career in management consulting. Contains information on skill requirements in consulting, key job areas, print resources and links to other Internet resources.

Jobs in Corporate Finance
http://www.cob.ohio-state.edu/dept/fin/jobs/corpfin.htm
An excellent site for those interested in a career in corporate finance. Insights into key job skills, requirements, job descriptions, salaries, and resources for more information.

The Monster Board
http://www.monster.com/
Information resources for HR professionals.

National Business Employment Weekly
http://www.nbew.com/
Job search and career guidance information.

Nijenrode Business Webserver
http://www.nijenrode.nl/nbr/career/
A site containing links to all types of online job opportunities and employment sites. Provides access to a wide range of Internet career search resources.

Online Career Center
http://www.occ.com
Over 250 companies post listings of employment opportunities. Listing is especially strong in the hi-tech area.